P9-AFI-451

N

LUZON

THE PHILIPPINES

PACIFIC OCEAN

MINDORO

SAMAR

PANAY

LEYTE

NEGROS   *BOHOL*

MINDANAO

▲ *MT. APO*

SULU ARCHIPELAGO

STRAIT

SULAWESI

MOLUCCAS

NEW GUINEA

BANDA SEA

LESSER SUNDAS

BAWA

FLORES

TIMOR

ARAFURA SEA

SUMBA

TIMOR SEA

SOUTHEAST ASIA

INDONESIA

BRUNEI

SINGAPORE

THE PHILIPPINES

THAILAND

MALAYSIA

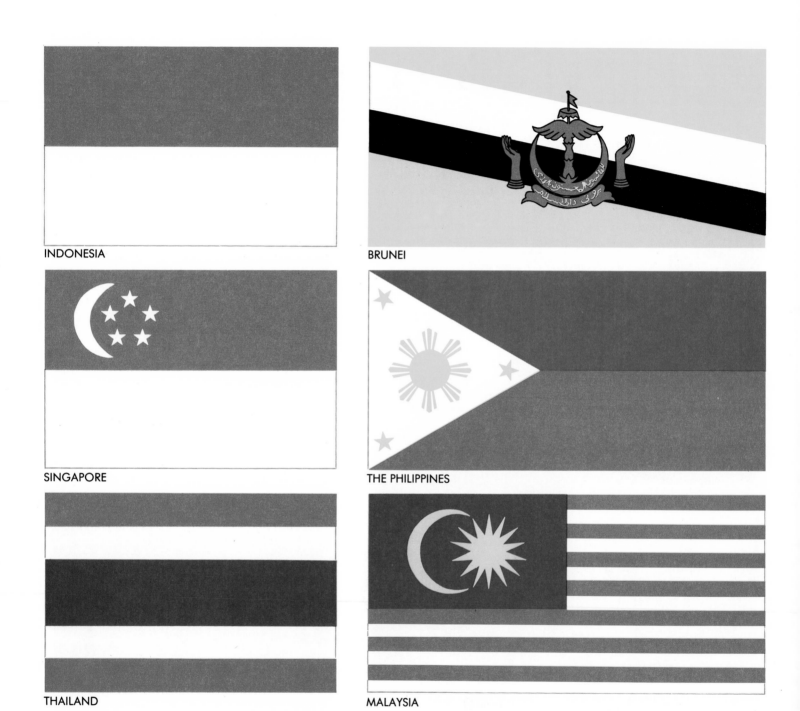

INDONESIA

BRUNEI

SINGAPORE

THE PHILIPPINES

THAILAND

MALAYSIA

SOUTHEAST ASIA

By the Editors of Time-Life Books
With photographs by Michael Freeman

TIME-LIFE BOOKS ∘ ALEXANDRIA, VIRGINIA

Other Publications

MYSTERIES OF THE UNKNOWN
TIME FRAME
FIX IT YOURSELF
FITNESS, HEALTH & NUTRITION
SUCCESSFUL PARENTING
HEALTHY HOME COOKING
UNDERSTANDING COMPUTERS
THE ENCHANTED WORLD
THE KODAK LIBRARY OF
  CREATIVE PHOTOGRAPHY
GREAT MEALS IN MINUTES
THE CIVIL WAR
PLANET EARTH
COLLECTOR'S LIBRARY OF THE CIVIL WAR
THE EPIC OF FLIGHT
THE GOOD COOK
WORLD WAR II
HOME REPAIR AND IMPROVEMENT
THE OLD WEST

This volume is one in a series of
books describing countries of the world—
their natural resources, peoples, histo-
ries, economies, and governments.

For information on and a full description of
any of the Time-Life Books series listed above,
please write:
Reader Information
Time-Life Customer Service
P.O. Box C-32068
Richmond, Virginia 23261-2068
Or call:
1-800-621-7026

Time-Life Books Inc.
is a wholly owned subsidiary of

TIME INCORPORATED

FOUNDER: HENRY R. LUCE 1898-1967

Editor-in-Chief: Jason McManus
Chairman and Chief Executive Officer: J. Richard Munro
President and Chief Operating Officer: N. J. Nicholas Jr.
Editorial Director: Ray Cave
Executive Vice President, Books: Kelso F. Sutton
Vice President, Books: George Artandi

TIME-LIFE BOOKS INC.

EUROPEAN EDITOR: Kit van Tulleken
Assistant European Editor: Gillian Moore
Design Director: Ed Skyner
Photography Director: Pamela Marke
Chief of Research: Vanessa Kramer
Chief Sub-editor: Ilse Gray

LIBRARY OF NATIONS

Series Editor: Tony Allan

Editorial Staff for *Southeast Asia*
Editor: Gillian Moore
Researcher: Susan Dawson
Designer: Lynne Brown
Design Assistant: Julie Busby
Sub-editor: Frances Dixon
Picture Department: Christine Hinze, Peggy Tout
Editorial Assistant: Molly Oates

EDITORIAL PRODUCTION

Coordinator: Nikki Allen
Assistant: Maureen Kelly
Editorial Department: Theresa John, Debra Lelliott

Contributors: The chapter texts were written by
James Clad, John Cottrell, Frederic V. Grunfeld,
Alan Lothian, and Andrew Turton.

Assistant Editor for the U.S. edition: Barbara Fairchild
Quarmby

CONSULTANT

Michael Williams is Senior Talks Writer
with the Far Eastern Service of the
British Broadcasting Corporation. His
Ph.D. thesis examined the early history of
Indonesian political movements in west
Java. He has traveled extensively in
Southeast Asia and written several studies
on the region's politics and history.

PHOTOGRAPHER

Michael Freeman began his photographic
career after studying geography at Oxford University. His pictures have appeared in many magazines and books,
including volumes in several Time-Life
Books' series. He is the author of a number of books on photography.

©1987 Time-Life Books Inc. All rights reserved. No
part of this book may be reproduced in any form or
by any electronic or mechanical means, including
information storage and retrieval devices or systems,
without prior written permission from the publisher,
except that brief passages may be quoted for reviews.

First Printing

Printed in U.S.A.
Published simultaneously in Canada.
School and library distribution by Silver Burdett
Company, Morristown, New Jersey.

TIME-LIFE is a trademark of Time Incorporated
U.S.A.

Library of Congress Cataloging in Publication Data
Southeast Asia.
  (Library of nations)
  Bibliography: p.
  Includes index.
  1. Asia, Southeastern. I. Freeman, Michael,
- 1945-   . II. Time-Life Books.
DS521.S675 1987   959   87-26722
ISBN 0-8094-5160-3
ISBN 0-8094-5161-1 (lib. bdg.)

Cover: In Zamboanga, a port in the southern
Philippines, the still sea reflects a waterfront mosque. Most of the Philippines were
converted to Roman Catholicism by Spanish
missionaries in the 16th century, but the southernmost islands remained loyal to Islam.

Front and back endpapers: A topographic
map illustrating the major islands, mountain
ranges, and rivers of Southeast Asia appears
on the front endpaper; the back endpaper
shows the six countries of the Association of
Southeast Asian Nations (ASEAN), and their
principal islands and towns.

CONTENTS

A REGION OF CONTRASTS

With a land area as large as India's and a population greater than the United States', the ASEAN countries form a major geopolitical group. In terms of territory and population, the giant is Indonesia, which is 3,000 times as big as Singapore. Indonesia is also the poorest, whereas Singapore's per capita GNP makes it comparable with Spain. Malaysia, with 16 million people, is the only country untroubled by overcrowding.

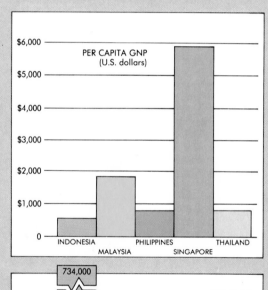

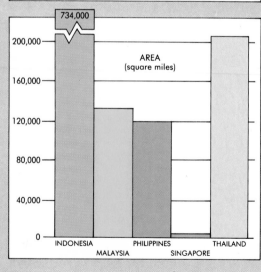

Traffic and shoppers crowd a street in the Chinatown district of Kuala Lumpur, the capital o

6

Malaysia. The Chinese are influential members of the trading community in many Southeast Asian cities.

ASSAULT ON THE WORLD'S OLDEST RAIN FORESTS

PERCENTAGE OF LAND AREA FORESTED

100
80
60
40
20
0

PHILIPPINES
BRUNEI
INDONESIA
SINGAPORE
THAILAND
MALAYSIA

The rain forests of Southeast Asia, the world's oldest, are surpassed in area only by those of Latin America. But they are being exploited at a rate that will consume them in a few decades if it continues unchecked. Pressure on resources is forcing farmers to clear virgin land for the plow, especially in Thailand, where the population has increased almost threefold in the past 50 years. Logging companies cull valuable hardwoods, including teak, ebony, and mahogany: Southeast Asia—including the ASEAN nations—supplies 70 percent of the tropical wood used worldwide. Conservation in the area is in its infancy, and few replanting projects are under way.

Wayfarers in the Malay Peninsula cross a bridge slung between densely wooded hillsides, where towering evergreens form a canopy over lesser

species. In their 30 million years of existence, Southeast Asia's rain forests have evolved a greater variety of flora than any other region in the world.

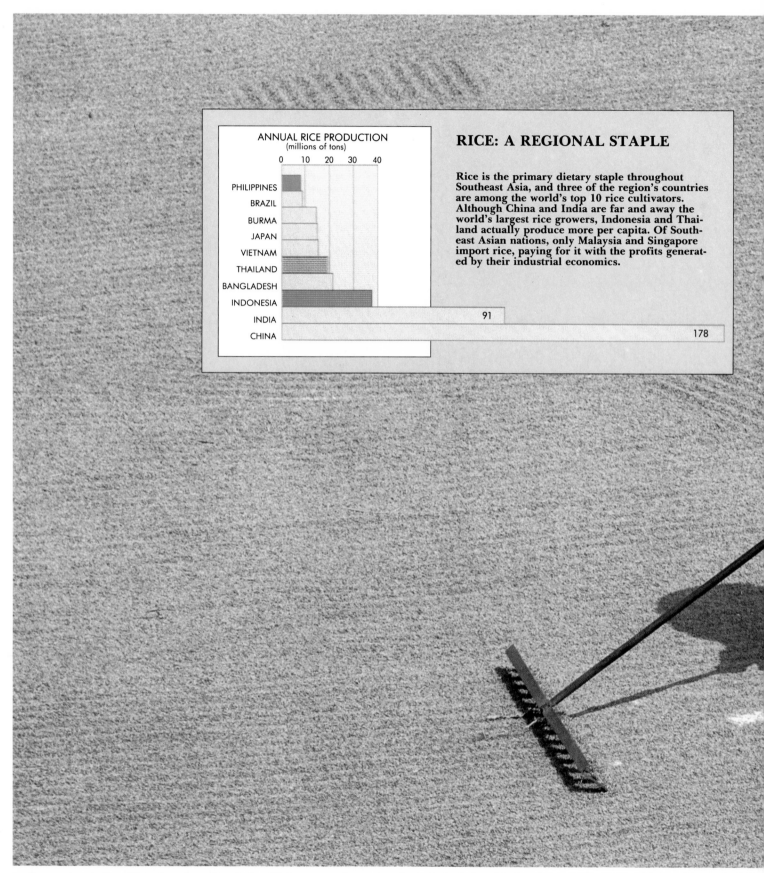

ANNUAL RICE PRODUCTION
(millions of tons)

	0	10	20	30	40

PHILIPPINES

BRAZIL

BURMA

JAPAN

VIETNAM

THAILAND

BANGLADESH

INDONESIA

INDIA — 91

CHINA — 178

RICE: A REGIONAL STAPLE

Rice is the primary dietary staple throughout Southeast Asia, and three of the region's countries are among the world's top 10 rice cultivators. Although China and India are far and away the world's largest rice growers, Indonesia and Thailand actually produce more per capita. Of Southeast Asian nations, only Malaysia and Singapore import rice, paying for it with the profits generated by their industrial economics.

In the courtyard of a mill upriver from Bangkok, a Thai woman rakes over unhusked rice being dried in the sun before it is milled and bagged. With

one sixth of the country devoted to paddy fields, Thailand is the world's largest exporter of rice, selling almost one quarter of its production abroad.

Brightly colored footwear covers the steps of a mosque in Brunei where Muslims have gathered for prayer. In both Brunei and Malaysia, Islam is the

state religion, and in Indonesia it is practiced by about 90 percent of the people—many of whom, however, retain some indigenous beliefs.

THE BOUNTY OF THE OCEANS

Scattered over innumerable islands and peninsulas, the seagoing peoples of Southeast Asia possess an invaluable resource in the 2,500 fish species that flourish in the surrounding tropical waters. Seafood is the region's major source of protein, and in most Southeast Asian countries, fish consumption is at least twice the world average.

Traditionally, local fishermen have gone out in sailing junks or outrigger canoes to make their catches with lines, traps, or drift nets. Much of the yield is then eaten fresh, although methods were long ago devised for preserving a surplus. The most characteristic means is fermentation, which yields a pungent sauce, but fish may also be smoked or dried.

Since the 1960s, however, the region's small fishermen have had to compete with a rapidly growing fleet of trawlers. The result has been an increased yield everywhere in the region; in Thailand, the catch rose tenfold in the dozen years prior to 1972, and a thriving export industry developed in frozen shrimp and squid, and canned tuna. Production has since leveled off, and there have been growing fears of overfishing.

Filipino fishing craft work the shallows near an island in the Sulu Archipelago, at the country's southern tip. The boats are motorized; the masts and

the webs of rope surrounding them serve to secure the outriggers, which give the vessels stability.

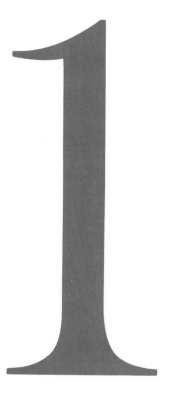

A RESOURCEFUL TROPICAL REGION

South of China, east of India: The description is at once vague and exotic. Southeast Asia is certainly the latter, at least to Western eyes: lush, tropical, the home of scores of ethnic groups and cultures. But the term is less vague than it once was; "Southeast Asia" has steadily acquired a more restricted meaning since the region first emerged as a political entity during World War II. At that time, the phrase was used in reference to a vast area: the great peninsula of Indochina, dangling like ripe fruit from the Asian landmass, and the enormous, equatorial archipelago to its south. Both of the regions were made up of many countries. In the jungle-clad highlands of the peninsula were Burma, Thailand, the Malay States, and French Indochina, which comprised the lands now known as Vietnam, Laos, and Kampuchea. The thousands of islands in the archipelago included New Guinea, Borneo, and the Philippines group.

Now, this broad geographical definition has largely been superseded by a more focused, geopolitical one. In this book, the term indicates specifically the six members of the Association of Southeast Asian Nations (ASEAN): Indonesia, Malaysia, Thailand, Singapore, the Philippines, and the sultanate of Brunei. The association was formed in 1967 as a defensive measure against the wars then plaguing Indochina.

For a quarter of a century before then, the conflict in Vietnam had dominated the politics of the region. First it was an anticolonial struggle against the French, then it was a war between the new states of North and South Vietnam. In the late 1950s, the American government was drawn in; the United States first sent troops to the conflict in 1965. Both Vietnams suffered terrible destruction, and at the end of the 1960s, the fighting spilled across the region's notoriously fluid borders, submerging Laos and Cambodia in chaos, death, and misery. The other Southeast Asian nations looked on in horror, fearful that the contagion might strike them, too. Burma retreated behind the curtain of "Buddhist Socialism" and kept to itself, Thailand and the Philippines allied themselves strongly with the United States, while Indonesia put its faith in the Nonaligned Movement.

When ASEAN was founded, few regarded it as a chance for the beginning of a new regional polity. The five founder nations—Brunei was not yet a member—shared anti-Communist sentiments and a laissez-faire approach to their economies; between them, however, lay a history of mutual bickering and even outright hostility. The Bangkok meeting that launched the association was strong on rhetoric and weak on substance, and no achievement of note marked the organization's early years. The best it managed was the Declaration of Concord in 1976, establishing a "Zone of Peace, Freedom, and Neutrality" in the area, without any

Amid the lush tropical vegetation of the Indonesian island of Bali, flooded terraces, newly planted with rice shoots, ascend a hillside. Rice is Southeast Asia's staple food, and the region's landscapes have been shaped over millennia by its cultivation.

17

hint of how that aim would be achieved.

Sometimes, though, a crisis can help to forge a community, and ASEAN did develop into a practical and cohesive force, spurred on precisely because of the region's lack of peace, freedom, and neutrality. The fall of Saigon, the South Vietnamese capital, in 1975 brought about the end of the Vietnam War, but the ASEAN countries were left with a dangerous new neighbor, whose army of one million soldiers and wealth of military equipment gave the association's leaders sleepless nights. The withdrawal of U.S. military forces from Indochina was matched by an increasing Soviet presence. At the same time, China was still uncomfortably close and remained unpredictable. Some of ASEAN's worst fears were realized in 1979 when Vietnam invaded Kampuchea and Hanoi's troops, preceded by hundreds of thousands of ref-

ugees, arrived on Thailand's doorstep.

By then, however, ASEAN had at last closed ranks. Its foreign ministers began to hold annual meetings and soon discovered that they could exercise far more diplomatic pressure jointly than they ever could individually. The late 1970s, for instance, were the years of the so-called boat people, the endless stream of refugees who fled Communist Vietnam—often with Hanoi's connivance—and who then placed an intolerable strain on the neighboring ASEAN economies. The ASEAN nations mounted an international campaign that garnered a twofold success: Vietnam grudgingly reduced the flood, and the major industrial nations recognized that refugee resettlement was a world problem, and not just a regional one. In response to the invasion of Kampuchea, ASEAN pursued a sustained diplomatic offensive; their ef-

forts reached a high point when the United Nations refused to recognize the Kampuchean government that was backed by Vietnam and continued its support of the government that had been overthrown by the Vietnamese. By flexing its muscles, the association had found its strength.

ASEAN is not a military alliance, although individual members usually work together willingly in that field. It is not even an economic alliance, along the lines of the European Economic Community; much lip service is paid to the idea of cooperation, but the member nations have yet to completely eliminate import duties on one another's goods, and less than 20 percent of their trade is within ASEAN. A few joint projects have been set up—notably a giant fertilizer plant in Indonesia—but for the most part, the member countries compete against one another to

Six faces represent some of the many ethnic groups in Southeast Asia. On the far left is a Bontoc, a member of a small tribal community in the Philippines. The elderly man is a Singaporean Chinese, the boy a Thai. The three women are all of Malay stock, though their nationalities differ.

export primary products to the rest of the world.

Essentially, ASEAN is a political alignment, a recognition of common interests by neighboring countries. Until the need for a measure of political unity became apparent, there seemed to be little to draw them together. In their geography, race, religion, and history, as well as their economies and their politics, the countries of Southeast Asia show some marked and keenly felt contrasts. Diversity, indeed, is one of the hallmarks of the region.

Indonesia is by far the biggest of the ASEAN countries in both area and population. It encompasses the world's largest archipelago—13,677 islands in all. Its most substantial territories are Sumatra, Kalimantan (the bulk of the island of Borneo), and Irian Jaya (the western half of the island of New Guin-

ea). Much of Indonesia is tropical rain forest and only thinly populated. But the volcanic, extremely fertile islands of Java and Bali support a population density that is one of the world's highest, and Indonesia's total population of more than 167 million is the fifth highest. The great majority of Indonesians are of Malay stock—small-statured, brown-skinned people who came to the islands from the Asian hinterland 5,000 years ago. Most Indonesians are Muslims, although there are also millions of Hindus, Christians, and members of other religious groups.

Long a Dutch colony, Indonesia declared independence in 1945. Since an attempted Communist coup in 1965, which was repressed savagely, the army has had a central role in government.

Indonesia's northern neighbor, the Philippines, is another enormous archipelago. Its population of almost 55 mil-

lion is scattered among 7,107 palm-fringed islands. Most Filipinos are of Malay stock, although they are not very closely related to the Malays of Indonesia. A large Chinese minority has intermarried extensively with the Malays.

The Philippines had the unique experience of being colonized twice: 300 years under Spain, which left most Filipinos Catholic, were followed by 50 years of American rule. Independence came in 1946. In 1965, Ferdinand Marcos was elected president, and from 1969 until his hurried departure in 1986, he was a virtual dictator.

Next largest after the Philippines is Thailand, whose more than 50 million people inhabit about 200,000 square miles on the Asian mainland. Although mountains guard Thailand in the north, its heartland is a fertile plain as flat as a calm sea. The Thais are of a different stock than the Malays; in fact,

19

they are closer to the Chinese in appearance, distinguishable from the Malays by lighter skin and almond-shaped eyes. Most Thais are Buddhists.

Thailand is unique in ASEAN because it has never been colonized by a foreign power. By a mixture of luck, timely internal reform, and skillful diplomacy, it managed to remain free of the European empires that carved up the region in the 19th century. The old, absolutist kingdom of Siam has become a constitutional monarchy—although, as in Indonesia, the army plays a key political role.

West Malaysia descends below Thailand and points straight into the Java Sea like a gently angled kris—the Malay sword with a scalloped blade. The only link between the Indonesian archipelago and the Indochinese mainland, the Malaysian federation also reaches 440 miles across the South China Sea to include East Malaysia—the states of Sabah and Sarawak on the northern part of Borneo, which between them make up 60 percent of the country.

Malaysia used to be a British colony; West Malaysia, previously known as Malaya, gained its independence in 1957, and the Borneo lands achieved it in 1963. Today, Malaysia is a democracy that has a curious kind of revolving monarchy: Each of the country's nine hereditary sultans holds office in turn for a five-year period.

A century ago, most of the population of Malaysia was Malay and Muslim. But in the late 1980s, the Malays made up only 47 percent of the total population of 16 million, thanks to the large numbers of Chinese and Indians introduced by the British in order to develop the economy. The large Chinese minority is heavily represented in the modernized, urban sector of the econ-

A Javanese woman in a traditional skirtlike sarong gets shelter from a downpour as she waits for a rickshaw. Monsoon winds bring heavy rain to much of Southeast Asia; nearly 80 inches fall annually on Java.

omy. Disparities in wealth and power cause some tension between the Malays and the Chinese—riots in 1969 claimed more than 200 lives—but a spirit of compromise generally prevails.

Impressive natural resources and a steadily growing manufacturing base have helped to give Malaysia a relatively high standard of living. Thailand, the Philippines, and Indonesia are all rated by the World Bank as "lower-middle income" countries, whereas Malaysia has graduated to "upper-middle income" status.

But the region's greatest economic success story is its smallest state, the island-city of Singapore. Built from scratch by the British in 1819, Singapore and its predominantly Chinese population became independent in 1965. Since then, the city-state has surged ahead under the authoritarian, but elected, rule of Lee Kuan Yew and his People's Action party. Its average annual economic growth rate of 7.4 percent from 1960 to 1982 was not only one of the highest in the world, but it lifted Singapore's per capita GNP to $5,910 by 1982—higher than those of

such countries as Spain and Greece.

Singapore's 2.5 million people grumble at Lee's sometimes heavy-handed ways—a speech in which he urged female university graduates to have more children in order to increase the average intelligence of the island's population was widely ridiculed—but there is little real dissent. The small republic is too proud of its record, its high-technology skills, and its reputation as the most dynamic city in Asia.

The countries of Southeast Asia, as different as they are from one another, also exhibit a great deal of internal diversity. The Malay populations of Indonesia and the Philippines are far from homogeneous: Over the centuries, they have fragmented into numerous societies, each with its own cultural traditions and languages. These two countries and Malaysia also house many communities of tribal peoples. Thailand is culturally more unified, but its mountains shelter a number of racial minorities: mainly seminomadic peoples who have migrated in the past 100 years from farther north. Everywhere except in the miniature state of Singapore, the contrast between city and countryside is astonishing. The ASEAN capitals are as cosmopolitan as any in the world, yet not far out of town live farmers, fishermen, and hunter-gatherers whose lives have hardly been touched by the 20th century.

It was never intended that ASEAN should forge a single unit from the diversity of Southeast Asia, and if attempted, such an effort would certainly fail. The association has, however, allowed its members to know and understand one another. Regular meetings, standing committees, and frequent cultural exchanges have all contributed to the slow but steady growth of a regional identity. ASEAN provides a framework for peace and stability—no more, perhaps, but certainly no less. It was largely the sense of security resulting from ASEAN membership that caused Brunei to join the association when it became independent of Britain in 1984. For the tiny, oil-rich state in northern Borneo, it was much colder outside.

As Singapore's Lee Kuan Yew put it at a 1983 meeting, ASEAN has reached the stage of *musyawarah*—a carefully chosen Indonesian word that translates roughly as "the dialogue leading to consensus." For all their differences, the peoples of Southeast Asia share a heartfelt desire for a common position. From the level of a simple village meeting to that of government policy making, Southeast Asians would rather reach some sort of general agreement, however long discussions may take, than push their own ideas on others by force or, indeed, by simple majority voting. Common throughout the region's societies, this mediative ability helps stabilize them in the face of internal upheavals and is now a key factor in promoting harmony within ASEAN.

All of the ASEAN governments, however authoritarian or democratic, reflect the tendency toward consensus. Ever since its independence, Malaysia's parliamentary democracy has produced a coalition government that represents all three of the country's main political parties, while in Thailand, military regimes succeed one another with

During a Hindu festival in Bali, shrines with symbolic-colored cloths fill a temple enclosure. Unlike the rest of Indonesia, which had largely converted to Islam by the 16th century, Bali has remained a stronghold of the older faith, celebrating religious holidays with splendid ritual.

1

scarcely any of the bloodshed and destruction seen in so many African and South American countries. But while the desire for consensus generally dampens any conflict, it does occasionally have its darker side. If the status quo is threatened by a force that cannot be incorporated into the framework of agreement, violence of the most savage kind can erupt. Such was the case in Indonesia in 1965. After the Communists failed to seize power, hundreds of thousands died in reprisals.

The desire for consensus did not develop without cause: It is reinforced by the region's whole way of life, which in turn is a consequence of the climate.

Very high rainfall makes rice an ideal crop, and the most productive method of rice cultivation requires the joint efforts of an entire village. The outcome of centuries of teamwork is a society in which everyone functions, willingly enough, within fairly tight conventions; there is a strong sense of mutual responsibility—and an equally strong sense of shame if obligations are not met—combined with deference to authority and deep mistrust of change.

The climate is remarkably similar everywhere in Southeast Asia: The temperature remains very close to 82° F. throughout the year, and a heavy monsoon rainfall lasts for at least six

months. In the latter part of the year, many places in the region have torrential downpours almost every day.

Rice thrives on the heat and the abundant rain, and it is the cultivation of rice that occupies most of Southeast Asia's farmers. In 1980, farmers made up 76 percent of the population in Thailand, 58 percent in Indonesia, 50 percent in Malaysia, and 46 percent in the Philippines. Therefore, although agriculture is no longer the main source of income, it is still by far the biggest employer everywhere, except in urban Singapore. Agriculture remains, as it always has, the great shaper of culture and outlook.

Rice has an almost mystical importance in Southeast Asia, where it has provided most of the daily nourishment for thousands of years. The majority of people eat very little else: a few drops of palm or coconut oil, some vegetables or chilies for flavoring, and—if they can afford it—a few fragments of fish for protein. (According to one Thai legend, when the universe was young, rice alone was sufficient. But with the steady increase in evil since those far-off days, other flavorings have become a regrettable necessity.) Through its predominance, rice has come to be seen as more than mere food; it represents well-being and even honor. Thus, to maintain one's self-respect and the respect of one's neighbors, three meals of white rice every day are, culturally speaking, mandatory; it would be shameful not to have a store of rice in the house at all times.

The remarkable grain can flourish in virtually every variant of Southeast Asian geography. There are three methods of rice cultivation, and at least one of them will suit most terrains. The first is shifting cultivation, also known as swidden agriculture or "slash-and-burn." Although it is surprising to think of rice growing in the forest today, slash-and-burn is by far the oldest way of growing the cereal; the relative importance of this shifting cultivation method may have diminished, but it is still practiced, especially by tribal groups, in sparsely populated areas.

The technique is rudimentary. Villagers simply cut down a few acres of forest, allow the dead wood to dry for a few months, and burn it. In the nutrient-rich ash, they plant their rice. After the harvest, they move to another place for the next crop and allow the forest to return to its natural state. The method has considerable advantages: Scarcely any equipment is required, and a modest amount of labor can yield a handsome return. But shifting cultivation has one great drawback: Because the forest requires at least nine years to regenerate itself, the method requires a lot of land. Should the population increase and farmers be tempted to shorten the interval that the land lies fallow, the result would always be the same. The fragile rain-forest soil loses nutrients faster than they can be replaced, yields fall disastrously, the farmers starve, and the forest ecology is ruined for years, perhaps forever.

The second method—broadcasting, or dry cultivation—uses established fields and necessitates plowing. It probably began when local population pressures started to make slash-and-burn impracticable. Large areas may be cleared—provided they are in river valleys or receive floodwaters—and in the dry season, they are plowed and seeded with deep-rooted rice varieties. The land itself is not the source of the rice plants' nourishment. This nourishment is instead derived from the rising floods of the rainy season: The waters that inundate the fields are rich in nutrients washed from upland forest soil. There is the expense of the draft animals and equipment, which the shifting cultivators do not need, but the method guarantees a higher yield from a given area of land.

Dry cultivation, which was historically important, is now practiced only in confined pockets. In most of Southeast Asia, a third method—transplanting, or wet-rice cultivation—has long been the norm. Rice seedlings are cultivated in nursery beds and then transplanted into fields and kept under water to just the right level. Water control is essen-tial, whether it involves carefully maintained dikes around a field that can hold seasonal rainfalls or enormously complex irrigation projects designed to tap and tame the floodwaters of a major river system. The labor costs of transplanting individual seedlings by hand are immense, especially in Java and parts of the Philippines, where water-retaining terraces ascend mountains almost to the clouds. But the benefits of wet-rice cultivation are also tremendous. Dikes give the cultivators the control that dry-rice farmers lack, and if the land is irrigated with a year-round supply of river water, wet-rice cultivation allows two or three crops in a year. Where the terrain is suitable, the method can support much larger populations than the more primitive methods—sometimes more than 1,000 people for each square mile.

In addition to the labor requirements, however, wet-rice cultivation demands a very high degree of social cooperation. First, the initial investment of energy and materials in making terraces, dikes, and ditches would be far beyond the resources of any one family group or even a small village. Second, the continuous maintenance required and the special efforts needed at certain times in the annual cycle—in transplanting and harvesting, for example—would be impossible without wholehearted agreement and application: without, in a word, consensus. Although wet-rice cultivation is much more efficient than the ancient slash-and-burn method in terms of the population it can support, it is also much more fragile. The wet-rice method requires a symbiotic relationship among the people that is even more intricate than the complex systems of water engineering that are its manifestation.

A pepper plantation cuts a swath through the dense jungle of Kalimantan—the Indonesian part of Borneo. Indonesia is the world's third-largest supplier of pepper, a spice that has drawn Europeans to Southeast Asia since the 16th century.

1

The traditions of consensus that wet-rice farming made imperative are reinforced by religious beliefs. Both Islam and Thai Buddhism put strong emphasis on the community, and religious festivals strengthen the villagers' sense of their common needs and goals.

At the village level, this concept works in a reasonably egalitarian way, with an emphasis on politeness and consideration for others. Villagers traditionally collaborate in house building, support the sick and unemployed in their community, and share any windfalls as well as the consequences of a bad harvest.

But the push toward consensus is anything but democratic in the Western sense; indeed, it operates largely by respect for authority. In a village meeting, for instance, everyone's concurrence in a decision will certainly be sought; but in practice, ordinary peasants are unlikely to raise their voices against the headman. Even the Communist party, when it was actively recruiting in Indonesian villages in the 1950s and 1960s, could not make any headway against traditional patterns of respect—although it did use them to its advantage. Instead of stirring up class feeling among the individual villagers, the recruiters went straight to the leader. If they could impress him by their policies, they knew he would bring his village into the party fold.

Throughout Southeast Asia, leaders are elected—after a fashion—by their fellow villagers. That is, only persons of a certain standing, usually relatively wealthy, will be selected; they will invariably be able to rely on the support of all those who work for them or have incurred some other obligation, and the election is likely to be uncontested. In fact, rather than call the process an election, it might be better to simply say that the leader is chosen after a period of discussion.

In spite of the ingrained conservatism of Southeast Asia, the roles of the village leaders are changing. In the past, particularly during the colonial period, the headmen were very much the villagers' representatives to higher authority. They would receive visitors from the outside world and, if necessary, journey to town to confer with the provincial authorities. Nowadays, however, they play a role as the government's representatives to the villagers—unpaid civil servants. They are expected to collect taxes on behalf of the central government and to organize military conscription.

Such an adaptation is only one example of the changes that are coming increasingly quickly to a society that is resistant to change. Change is most obvious in the cities, of course, with their new industries, their skyscrapers, their bustle—and their astonishing growth. Each of the region's three largest cities—Bangkok, Manila, and Jakarta—is fast becoming a megalopolis. According to projections, the 16.6 million people who are expected to live in Jakarta by the year 2000 will make it the world's 10th-largest city. About 10 percent of Thailand's population lives in Bangkok; an even larger proportion of the Philippines' population lives in Manila.

Although it may be less obvious, the more important change may be occurring in the countryside, because that is where most Southeast Asians live. Much rural change has been the result of the so-called Green Revolution—the combination of improved crop strains, new farming techniques, and modern equipment that is transforming large parts of the developing world. The improvements it has produced have resulted in a general increase in prosperity and more food for everyone, but there have been profound cultural effects as well. The rich have benefited most, since it is they who have money to invest in fertilizers and equipment; the gap between successful and unsuccessful farmers is wider than ever. Success, in turn, breeds a certain capitalist frame of mind, which runs directly against traditions of consensus.

In Java, for example, villagers used to harvest rice with old-fashioned, inefficient knives that left a sizable proportion of grain behind. It was not wasted, however: Its gleaning served as payment for the local landless poor who had helped with the harvest. Now, farmers use better and more costly equipment that clears the fields efficiently; the process suits the more money-conscious owners, but weakens the ties of mutual support that bind the village together. Indeed, a prosperous farmer will often use workers from a village 18 or more miles away; they will be paid in a straightforward and contractual fashion, with none of the complex social obligations that would be incurred if the field hands were recruited among the farmers' own neighbors.

Yet the old ways are not going to vanish overnight. Deference, politeness, and the desire for agreement are deeply embedded in cultures as superficially different as Buddhist Thailand, the Christian Philippines, and Muslim Indonesia. The attitudes are derived from the land itself and the manner by which, for centuries, it has been worked. They are native in a way that even the great faiths that have entrenched themselves in the area are not. The Indonesians—who describe the whole complex code of customary

THE SULTANATE OF OIL

The 2,226-square-mile state of Brunei, made up of two adjacent enclaves on Borneo's north coast, is awash with oil. Thanks to the oil and natural gas that account for 99 percent of its exports, Brunei's per capita GNP is the world's third highest.

Most of the wealth is at the disposal of the sultan—the last of Asia's absolute rulers—who lives in luxury, but who has invested oil revenue in health care and education, which benefits the populace at large.

Malays—most of whom work the land—make up two thirds of the state's 220,000 population. Another 20 percent are ethnic Chinese, who dominate business life. Their status is precarious, however, for Brunei is strongly Islamic, and most non-Muslims are denied citizenship.

Brunei converted to Islam in the 15th century. For a time, Brunei ruled much of Borneo, but its power later declined, and in 1888, it became a British protectorate. Already an oil producer in 1963, when Britain's other Borneo lands merged with Malaya, Brunei chose to retain its status rather than dilute its prosperity by joining the new nation. It became independent in 1984.

The glittering dome of a modern mosque towers over the watery heart of Brunei's capital, Bandar Seri Begawan.

behavior with the deceptively short word *adat*—have a saying that acknowledges this truth: "Religion comes in from the sea, but *adat* comes down from the mountains."

Since the sea has had a crucial impact on the societies of the area, the first half of that Indonesian proverb has almost as much significance as the second. Three of the ASEAN countries are island states, and the others all have ex-

tensive coastlines. The Chinese have long recognized the significance of this: Their name for what the West calls Southeast Asia, Nan Yang, translates literally as "the South Sea." Within Southeast Asia, the sea is the natural route between communities, fish is a major resource, and boating skills are universal. And because of the area's position at the maritime crossroads where the Indian Ocean and the Pacific Ocean meet, it has been one of the world's

most cosmopolitan places for centuries.

The ocean highways brought traders, and with them inevitably came ideas. The first foreign precepts that notably influenced the region came from India in the form of Hinduism and Buddhism—but like everything else that came to Southeast Asia, both of them were adapted to suit the needs of local societies. Hinduism, for instance, arrived almost 2,000 years ago and spread rapidly over most of the region; the people accepted the Hindu pantheon—as well as the skilled administrative services of the Indian Brahmins who proselytized the new religion—but they never adopted the caste system that stratifies Indian society. Today, the Hindu heritage is apparent in the rituals of the Malaysian and Thai courts as well as in the folklore and dramatic arts of the entire region. Other, more aggressive faiths, however, have long since converted most of the religion's adherents. Only on the Indonesian island of Bali is Hinduism still widely practiced. Even there, it is very different from the Indian version: One of the foremost ways that an Indian Hindu practices his religion is by following exactly his particular caste's rules for daily life, whereas the Balinese, lacking India's strict division into castes, are much less constricted in their behavior.

Similarly, Buddhism, which spread from India in the seventh century, underwent a few sea changes before it developed into Thailand's national religion. Today, it coexists with the country's indigenous religious practices, such as the veneration of the Rice Mother: the spirit of the grain.

India's contribution to Southeast Asian culture was always qualified by strong trading links with China, but the next cultural influence to rock the region dramatically came not from the north but from far to the west. The confident message of Islam was brought by Arab merchants to coastal communities in Southeast Asia as early as 1250. It took firm root in the 15th century with the conversion of the ruler of Malacca, a mighty, though short-lived empire extending over Malaya and a good part of Sumatra. In the next two centuries, Islam spread outward from the Malay Peninsula, supported by Malaccan power and carried by Malaccan ships throughout the Southeast Asian archipelago as far as Mindanao, now a part of the southern Philippines. Islam made only limited headway in Buddhist Thailand and the neighboring territory, but almost everywhere else it was accepted with enthusiasm.

It still is. Perhaps Islam's simplicity appealed to men and women who were tired of the hierarchic Hindu world view; perhaps its fatalism struck a chord with tropical peoples noted for their easygoing natures. At any rate, present-day Indonesia has the world's largest Muslim population, and Islam is in the Malaysian Constitution: To be a Malay in Malaysia is, officially, to be a Muslim. Brunei, too, is solidly Islamic, and all the other countries have Muslim minorities, often substantial.

Islam in Southeast Asia is rarely the militant, fire-and-sword faith of the Arabian Peninsula and the Middle East. Like Hinduism and Buddhism before it, it has been "tropicalized" into something a good deal gentler and more flexible. Extreme views do exist, however. During Indonesia's struggle to gain independence, a movement called Darul Islam—literally, "The House of Islam"—took up arms to establish an Islamic state. It was put down but never eliminated completely. In the Philippines, too, militant Muslims sometimes add to the government's security problems. And in Malaysia, which apart from Brunei is the most orthodox Muslim country of Southeast Asia, fundamentalism is growing. But most Southeast Asians—though certainly devout, as the large numbers who make a pilgrimage to Mecca attest—are simply not single-minded enough to be fanatical.

More than 250 years after Islam reached Southeast Asia, the Europeans began arriving. They were drawn initially by the immensely lucrative spice trade, but they stayed to build empires: The boundaries of the modern nations of Southeast Asia result from the caprice and design of competing European powers. Each imperial ruler placed its own distinctive mark on the territory under its sway.

The Portuguese were the first Europeans on the scene. They were soon ousted by the Dutch from most of their trading stations, but they retained a solitary foothold—East Timor, in the Indonesian archipelago—right up until 1975, thus becoming the last colonial power to leave Southeast Asia.

Even before the Dutch arrived, the Spanish had begun annexing the Philippines. Unlike the other European intruders, they attempted—and achieved—wholesale conversion of the native peoples to their religion. To this day, 85 percent of Filipinos are Roman Catholics. The Spaniards also gave the Philippines its name, in honor of their king, Philip II.

At the end of the 18th century, the British established a foothold on an island off the Malay Peninsula and subsequently expanded their influence. In the course of the next century, they came to control most of what would become Malaysia, Singapore, and Brunei; the Dutch established their hold on Indonesia, and the Spanish remained firmly ensconced in the Philippines. Among the ASEAN countries, only Thailand retained its independence.

Toward the end of the 19th century, the European colonizers controlling most of the region systematically began to exploit the region's resources. They introduced new crops and employed unfamiliar agricultural methods to create the most lucrative plantation economies the world has ever seen. Only the Europeans had the funds to clear whole sections of forest, replant scientifically, and then endure the profitless years until the new trees were old enough to produce a harvest. Their efforts changed the face of Southeast Asia and had repercussions that are still being felt today.

Although spices had drawn the Europeans to the area initially, tobacco, sugar, and coffee overtook them in value by the late 19th century, and two extraneous crops joined the region's native mainstays. One was the oil palm, a native of West Africa, the fruit of which yields oil for margarine and soap. The Dutch had introduced it into Sumatra on an experimental basis as early as 1848, but it was many years before demand for the crop's derivatives built up to a spectacular level. The other novelty, rubber, took off much more rapidly.

Rubber trees originally grew wild in Brazil's Amazon jungle, and until the late 19th century, supply of the small quantities used by the world's markets was a Brazilian monopoly. But in 1876, an enterprising British botanist smuggled seeds back to England, where they were made to germinate in the Royal Botanic Gardens at Kew, near London. Seedlings were sent to Ceylon and to Singapore, reaching Malaya in the 1890s—to coincide with the arrival of the automobile industry in Europe and the United States. Production of pneumatic tires sent demand for the commodity spiraling upward. Within a decade, rubber was Malaya's most valuable export, and rubber trees were being planted in Java, Sumatra, Borneo: anywhere they could be made to grow.

The prime sites for plantations were almost always in thinly populated areas. In Malaysia, self-sufficient peasants had no desire to uproot themselves in order to work on the plantations, and the British preferred not to interfere with their traditional societies. The Dutch partially solved the problem of

In the 1640s, a merchant of the Dutch East India Company, with his wife, points proudly to company ships at Batavia (now Jakarta).

the labor shortage in Sumatra by transplanting Malays from Java, which was overcrowded. The shortage elsewhere was made up by importing workers from afar. The British shipped Indians by the millions to labor in Malaysia; British and Dutch alike opened their ports to a flood of Chinese. Unwittingly—or at any rate without much concern—Western developers had precipitated one of history's great migrations, comparable with the movement of European peoples across the Atlantic to the United States.

Many of the newcomers came only as contracted laborers, committed to return to their homelands with their meager savings after a few years' work, but millions stayed. The inevitable racial tensions were exacerbated by the fact that the Asian middle class that emerged in the colonial period—managers and middle managers, and not a few extremely prosperous merchants and shipowners—tended to be recruited from the immigrant Chinese and Indian communities.

Imperialist energy and the new racial leavening undoubtedly worked economic wonders. By the 1930s, Southeast Asia as a whole was providing the bulk of the tropical produce bought and sold on the world's markets: 75 percent of the copra, for example, and 55 percent of the palm oil. The region produced 93 percent of the world's rubber, and Malaya alone yielded 60 percent of the tin.

But colonial development had its drawbacks. The main one, from the point of view of the colonized countries, was that most of the wealth produced disappeared into the coffers of the imperial powers. Part of it went into improving health care and sanitation throughout the region, which caused a marked rise in life expectancy; wages, however, remained low. Moreover, the emphasis on exports led to economies that were rich in certain areas and entirely neglected in others.

Throughout the region, the local educated elite came to resent foreign rule and to envy the rulers their opportu-

Palms front the city of Cebu's cathedral, one of many baroque churches built by the Spanish during their 300-year rule over the Philippines.

29

1

nities. In the fast-growing and half-modern cities of the early 20th century, nationalism was in the air.

The currents were felt among the new administrative class even in Thailand, which had never been colonized. Trained to serve faithfully as the stewards of an enlightened despot, the bureaucrats grew jealous of the king's absolute power. The result was a coup in 1932 that constitutionalized the absolute monarchy.

. The nationalists in other regions also had their chance, far sooner than they had expected. The Japanese onslaught in World War II swept Western rule from Southeast Asia in six brief months, boosted Asian morale, and destroyed European prestige. Most nationalists welcomed the takeover and collaborated with the Japanese, who in turn granted many of them limited self-government and even raised small local armies. Although it became clear that Japanese rule was just as oppressive and far more brutal than the European dominion it had replaced, it did give nationalists a taste of power. When Japan's short-lived Greater East Asian Coprosperity Sphere collapsed in turn in 1945, it was clear that there could be no return to the prewar status quo. Over the next two decades, all the territories which later became ASEAN members were granted independence.

Since the war, all of the ASEAN countries have had to face similar problems. All had economies designed to supply the needs of far-off Western markets. All had a serious shortage of trained personnel, especially scientists, technologists, and engineers. All had to accommodate ethnic minorities, some of substantial size. All had to face a tide of rising expectations among their popu-

lations, and the likelihood of dangerous political problems if these expectations remained unfulfilled—the threat was heightened because only Thailand could rely on a long tradition of national cohesion. Most of these problems were the result of colonialist policies. They have all had to be dealt with during a period of rapid population growth—the outcome of the successful reduction of death rates achieved during the colonial era.

Compared with most of the Third World, ASEAN has done well. Indeed, from the mid-1970s to the mid-1980s, it grew faster than any other group of developing countries. All the ASEAN nations except Brunei have established some manufacturing capability: Brunei is still completely dependent on imports for its basic requirements, but with an oil-supported per capita income of $21,000 a year, its people can

afford them. Many of the region's industries are joint ventures with foreign multinational corporations, usually either American or Japanese: Automobile plants are located in Thailand and the Philippines, for instance, and tires are produced in Indonesia. Malaysia has a major plant for the manufacturing of all types of vehicles—the federation has tried to reduce the influence of Western and Japanese capital on its economy—and it produces a significant proportion of the world's computer microchips. Singapore will build anything that will fit onto the busy little island.

For the time being, however, minerals and commodity crops remain crucial. Five of the six ASEAN member nations still rely on minerals and other primary products for the bulk of their exports, while the sixth—Singapore—depends on trading them. For Malaysia, the rubber and tin that helped to

30

keep the British Empire solvent are no longer of such importance; their prime position has been taken by oil, timber, and palm oil. Indonesia has the same range of commodities—and the fertile, volcanic soils of Java as well. The Philippines is blessed with copper and gold. Thailand has its fertile Chao Phraya delta and is developing an offshore gas field in the Gulf of Thailand.

In every country, a serious effort has been made to develop the most basic resource of all: the people. By the 1980s, primary education was virtually universal throughout all the ASEAN countries except Thailand, and secondary school enrollments ranged from 29 percent in Thailand to 65 percent in Singapore.

Education, however, has not been an unrelieved blessing, especially at the higher levels. Only a fraction of the students choking the big universities and institutes of learning in such cities as Bangkok and Manila will find jobs in technological areas. The rest will have to find work in the bureaucracies, or settle for menial jobs or even unemployment, where their disappointment could turn to dangerous discontent.

Of all Southeast Asia's various ethnic groups, none is more passionate about education than the Chinese. The Chinese should probably be seen as one of the region's most valuable resources. Dynamic, entrepreneurial, and often distrusted throughout the region, they control a disproportionate share of regional trade and industry—where they are not specifically excluded from it by legislation. The Chinese are active participants in all the professions, are generally better off than members of other Southeast Asian ethnic groups (although many Chinese are abysmally poor), and are feared as well as respect-

JAPAN'S WAR OF CONQUEST

Within hours of entering World War II on December 7, 1941, Japan launched an all-out assault on Southeast Asia. Surprise air attacks on the Philippines and Singapore were followed by an almost unopposed invasion of Malaya and then Singapore, which surrendered in February 1942. Troops also landed in the Dutch East Indies and the Philippines, which fell, after brave resistance, on March 9 and April 9, respectively. After an offensive of just 122 days, the Japanese were masters of the entire region.

Except in Singapore, where air raids killed hundreds, few civilians in Southeast Asia were scarred by Japan's lightning strike. But the three-year occupation that followed brought a heavy toll of suffering. While Europeans were herded into prison camps and forced labor, Japanese secret police terrorized local populations, and economic chaos caused many to starve.

A Singaporean mother grieves over her child, killed in a Japanese air raid.

ed for their commercial acumen.

The Chinese are scattered throughout the region, and because they almost invariably live in the big cities, they give the impression to the traveler of being more numerous than they are. Their numbers in fact range from 3 percent of the population in Indonesia, about 8 percent in Thailand, 20 percent in Brunei, 32 percent in Malaysia, to 76 percent in Singapore. In the Philippines, less than 2 percent of the population is of pure Chinese stock, but the proportion with some Chinese ancestry is much higher.

The legal status of the Chinese varies from country to country, from the full citizenship extended to them—a little grudgingly—in Malaysia, to the state of official nonexistence in which they live in Brunei, where only Muslims are citizens. The Chinese occupy a position, in fact, much like that of Europe's Jews throughout most of European history: a people accused of clannishness and suspected of alien loyalties, who are frequently blamed for every misfortune; nevertheless, they are often acknowledged as being creative, industrious, and virtually indispensable. In Thailand and the Philippines, marriage is helping to integrate them, but such mixed marriages are virtually unknown in the Muslim societies of Malaysia and Indonesia.

The dominant role of the Chinese in trade and commerce is beginning to diminish now, not only because of laws in most countries that limit their participation, but because Malays, Thais, Filipinos, and Indonesians are learning the business skills that have traditionally been Chinese. The proportion of Chinese in the population at large is likely to shrink as well, simply because of their relatively low birthrate: As a group, the Chinese community has already crossed over the threshold into the relative affluence that helps to limit the birthrate.

In most of Southeast Asia, though, the pressure of rising populations is still a serious problem. Once again, Indonesia provides the most dramatic example. A 1905 census counted 38 million people in the area of the present nation; there were more than 80 million by the 1950s, 153 million in 1982, and it is estimated that there will be 212 million by the year 2000. The projections for Thailand and the Philippines are almost as high. Land in these three countries is becoming scarce, although Malaysia has room to spare.

The population problem is one that the region's governments take very seriously indeed. Most are engaged in sophisticated family-planning campaigns, and Indonesia also runs a program of assisted resettlement from Java, which is extremely overcrowded, to outlying islands where there is empty land. Prosperity—which in demographic terms is the most effective contraceptive of all—is beginning to have an effect. But, except in Singapore, birthrates have not declined enough to match the decrease in death rates.

In a sense, the ASEAN countries are in a race to get rich before their surging populations condemn them to poverty. Given the enterprising nature of the people, the economic growth they have achieved so far, and the growing harmony in the region, the prospects seem bright. Although ASEAN will not of itself promote the growth its members need, the existence of the association does allow its members to pursue their own policies in peace. Lee Kuan Yew's "dialogue leading to consensus" is well under way. □

A mission helicopter draws curious onlookers from their huts in the misty highlands of Irian Jaya, Indonesia's eastern-most territory. Until air contact was established in the past few decades, many Irianese lived a secluded Stone-Age existence.

An offering at a Balinese festival, featuring the head of the Hindu demon Bhoma, serves to ward off the spirit's evil presence. Made entirely of vividly colored rice dough, the offering stands taller than a man; it typifies Indonesian art in its swirling lines and intricate detail.

A REPUBLIC OF ISLANDS

The world's sixth-largest and fifth most-populous nation is no older than a bold proclamation willing it into existence on August 17, 1945. The Republic of Indonesia's Declaration of Independence signaled the end of more than three centuries of Dutch dominion, but only after four years of warfare did the Dutch reluctantly agree to leave the country. In December 1949, Indonesian sovereignty became a reality.

A major geopolitical power had been created. Its essential stability, in contrast with so many emerging countries, is attested to by a tally of its presidents: There have been only two, in more than 40 years of independence. Today, large foreign-embassy staffs closely monitor the international relations of Jakarta, Indonesia's capital, one of Asia's strategic centers. Multinational corporations invest billions of dollars in an economy that boasts an impressive range of resources, including the largest known oil and gas reserves in non-Communist Asia. Nearby Malaysia and Brunei acknowledge their neighbor as both the cultural and political center of the Malay world.

It would have taken uncommon prescience to predict a bright future for Indonesia, because the country hardly looked like a natural political unit when it first emerged as an independent nation. Indonesia is made up of 13,677 islands strewn across more than 3,000 miles of tropical seas—a span that exceeds the distance from California to Florida, or from Ireland to eastern Turkey. Many of these islands are no more than rocky outcrops, and only 8 percent of them are permanently inhabited; however, that small proportion includes most of Borneo, the world's third-largest island, and half of New Guinea, the second largest.

The galaxy of islands encompasses endless diversity. The climate is wettest in the west, and some of the eastern islands are quite arid. And the vegetation changes accordingly, from the dense rain forests of Kalimantan—Indonesian Borneo—to the dusty savannas of Timor. Ethnically, too, there are differences coincident with longitude and latitude. In the western islands, most people have the brown skin, straight hair, and distinctive features of the typical Malay. Toward the east, most notably in Irian Jaya—western New Guinea—many people have the tightly curled hair, dark skin, and blunter features of the Melanesians, a group scattered across the South Pacific. Within these two broad categories is a mosaic of ethnic groups, made more complex by a vast array of traditional and modern life-styles and 250 distinct languages.

Superficially, Indonesia's diverse and scattered peoples might appear to have little in common beyond the experience of having been ruled by the Dutch. The boundaries of the Dutch possession certainly determined the parameters of Indonesia, but the country is far from an artificial creation. The islands had a long history of contact with one another; among the coastal peoples, in particular, a high coincidence of custom and ritual had developed. A succession of empires based in Java and Sumatra had extended their influence over other parts of the archipelago. Beginning with the advent of Islam in the 13th century, religion became a powerful bond. Despite the survival of many animist and mystical beliefs, nearly 90 percent of Indonesians follow Islam, giving the country by far the largest Muslim population in the world today.

The Dutch strengthened these tentative bonds by imposing an administrative unity on the archipelago. They also inadvertently contributed to the nationalist cause: By providing a common focus for resentment, they drew the islanders together.

The Javanese have long been the most numerous of Indonesia's populations, and they were prominent in the independence movement that gathered strength in the 1920s and 1930s. Had they tried to impose a specifically Javanese stamp on the movement, they might easily have caused a rift that would have split Indonesia into two or more countries. But they were wise enough not to antagonize other islanders. They refrained, for example, from promoting their own language. Javanese would, in any case, have been unsuitable for a modern nation. Developed in the hierarchic world of the Javanese courts, it employs three distinct vocabularies that allow speakers to define their social status as superior, equal, or inferior to that of the listener.

Seeking a more egalitarian means of communication, the nationalists hit upon "market Malay," which, for centuries, had been the lingua franca of

2

traders and sailors throughout the archipelago. The language was unsullied by class consciousness and acceptable to all Indonesians because it was not associated with a particular group. Now called *bahasa Indonesia*—the Indonesian language—the tongue is the envy of other large and heterogeneous countries, such as India. It is the language of officialdom and the means of instruction in all secondary schools; it dominates the media and the streets of the principal cities. It is even understood in the villages, although people continue to speak their own languages.

With a common language to help strengthen the bonds of a joint colonial past and a religion shared by the vast majority, Indonesia has achieved a powerful sense of nationhood. The sentiment is not quite universal, however. In Irian Jaya and East Timor—two latecomers that were coerced into Indonesia in 1963 and 1975, respectively—widespread resentment of the annexations still finds expression in simmering guerrilla conflict. But elsewhere, secessionist movements are virtually nonexistent. The nation can display with justification its motto Unity in Diversity.

A tour of Indonesia's ample sweep begins most naturally near the core—the so-called inner islands of Java, Bali, and Lombok, which possess the most fertile soils in the world. The islands owe their lushness to regular monsoon rains and to a chain of volcanoes stretching along their length. Many of the volcanoes are active, and although their eruptions occasionally bring disaster on an awesome scale, the eruptions also have a beneficial effect: Gray volcanic ash, full of chemical nutrients, enriches the soil to such an extent that even wooden fence

A poster commemorating Indonesia's Declaration of Independence from the Dutch in 1945 portrays the two leading campaigners for freedom, Sukarno *(left)* and Hatta *(right)*. They became Indonesia's first president and vice president, respectively.

posts sometimes sprout and grow into an impenetrable thicket within a couple of years.

All three islands cultivate rice intensively, and the ordered landscapes that result, especially in the small but varied compass of Bali, are reminiscent of a lovingly tended English garden. In some places, the flooded paddy fields reflect the azure sky; elsewhere, the land is a patchwork of greens, as adjacent plots ripen a day or two apart. On steep slopes, mountains are carved into giant, curving terraces, above which emerge the imposing volcanic peaks.

With their extraordinary fertility, the inner islands can support a vast multitude. A staggering 100 million people live on Java, a territory only a little larger than New York State. Its population accounts for nearly two thirds of all Indonesians and one third of the entire population of ASEAN. The numerical superiority of the Javanese regularly brings them to the fore in Indonesian life. Java, whose courtly culture has defined Indonesia's national heritage, has historical claims to preeminence as the

focal point of the early kingdoms. Later, as a colony, Java became the main base of the Dutch.

Batavia, the Dutch political headquarters on Java's north shore, was renamed Jakarta and is now the capital—a city that, according to predictions, will be one of the largest in the world by the 21st century. Despite attempts in the 1970s to close Jakarta to newcomers, it still acts as a magnet for rural migrants, who could swell today's population of eight to nine million to 20 million by the year 2000. No one—not even the city government—knows how many people actually live in the sprawl of red-tiled houses that stretches from the mouth of the heavily polluted Ciliwung River to the exclusive housing development raised by speculators along the former paddy fields at the city's southern edge.

For the lucky few, there are all the diversions that money and influence can buy. Four-star hotels line the main Jalan Thamrin Boulevard. Golf clubs, amusement centers, and luxury-goods shops dot the wealthy southern suburbs. Oil money has created a subclass of nouveaux riches who often shop in Singapore on weekends and travel to Amsterdam four or five times a year. Wealthy Chinese businessmen live in splendor, albeit behind closed doors, and the pampered children of top government officials and army personnel are taken to school in chauffeur-driven automobiles.

About one third of Jakarta's citizens, however, live in desperate poverty in squalid squatter communities that lack virtually all amenities. Some of these settlements—earthen-floored huts jammed into shallow recesses among the larger commercial developments—have housed two generations of poor. Most of their inhabitants live a hand-

In Jakarta, the capital of Indonesia, a broad avenue cuts through an infinity of modest, red-tiled buildings—many of them the homes and workplaces of small tradespeople. With few high-rise buildings, Jakarta retains its village atmosphere, despite its population of more than eight million.

to-mouth existence by peddling cigarettes, shining shoes, or scavenging.

With all life spilling into the streets, Jakarta's frenzy never pauses. In the narrow streets, three-wheeled taxis, motorcycles, badly dented buses, and pedicab drivers hustling for customers create a perpetual cacophony, while at night one enclave or another is sure to offer a street spectacle to celebrate a local boy's circumcision or a wedding.

Despite Jakarta's frenetic rate of growth, two thirds of Java's inhabitants are still rural folk—fishermen putting out to sea in lateen-rigged outriggers or peasants heading toward their rice fields at four in the morning. A village typically comprises bamboo and palm-leaf houses, many of them with tiny courtyards. Here, life still moves to the rhythm of the soil—the cycle of planting, irrigating, draining, harvesting, and threshing.

But the tempo is quickening even in Java's rural heartland. New roads, inexpensive motorcycles, and efficient radio communications have made the capital less remote, both conceptually and geographically, than it was 10 years ago. Every village now has its own primary school, and 2,500 health centers scattered across the island have greatly increased a child's chances of survival.

This last change, desirable as it is, has been an important factor in Java's spiraling population, which rose from 76 million in 1971 to 91 million in 1980, when 50 percent of Javanese were under 17. Bali has seen a similarly rapid increase. The government introduced a nationwide birth-control campaign in 1970, which helped to reduce Indonesia's population growth rate from 2.7 percent in 1970 to 2.1 percent in 1985. Despite the deceleration, widely regarded as one of the Third World's

At dawn, pilgrims make their way along a mountain ridge toward the volcanic cone of Java's Mount Bromo to pay homage to the fire-god they believe inhabits its crater. Indonesia is studded with more than 400 volcanoes, of which some 70 are a known threat to the population.

greatest family-planning successes, Indonesia's population still increases by nearly 1.5 million people a year.

As the populations of Java and Bali have grown, the peasants have pushed higher up the volcanic slopes, abandoning wet-rice farming for dry-rice cultivation. In the process, they have felled large areas of forest for farmland and fuel, exposing soil to erosion.

Even with the new fields that have been hacked out of the forests, only about one quarter of the population of these two islands owns a substantial plot of land, and large numbers of landless laborers find work wherever they can. The government's answer to the problem is to resettle villagers from Java and Bali on the sparsely populated islands of Sumatra, Kalimantan, Sulawesi, and Irian Jaya. In the course of the 1979-1984 five-year plan, the government relocated 500,000 families—more than two million people. Offering the prospect of a free plot, house, and tools as an alternative to destitution, the project had more applicants than it could manage. But many of the relocated villagers came across unexpected difficulties in their new surroundings, which were generally far less fertile than the soils they were accustomed to tilling. Even the authorities admit that finding worthwhile virgin sites will become increasingly difficult. Relocation also runs into opposition among the host islanders, who sometimes find themselves outnumbered by the newcomers.

Although much of the enormous island of Sumatra consists either of mangrove swamp or of rolling hills with poor soil, a rich alluvial plain in the northeast provides a prime area for cultivation. Sumatra is not burdened with a vast population, and plantations in this re-gion have produced export crops—chiefly tobacco, rubber, and oil palms—since the 19th century. The island is also blessed with mineral wealth. It has been an important source of tin beginning in the last century, and in recent years, most of Indonesia's oil and gas has been found off its shores. Thanks to its bountiful resources, Sumatra is Indonesia's economic mainstay, pulling in about 70 percent of the nation's export income.

To many of the ethnic groups scattered among the island's mountains and coastal reaches, such a statistic means little. They practice subsistence farming and may see little of the outside world. Sumatra's peoples include some of the most devout Muslim populations in Indonesia. And the Acehnese of the island's northernmost tip, known for their determined resistance to Dutch hegemony, formed an Islamic stronghold that fought the Dutch right up to the 20th century; today, they have been granted some autonomy in recognition of their independent spirit.

Kalimantan, more than 300 miles east of Sumatra, is Indonesia's largest territory and one of the world's most extensive tracts of primeval rain forest. Its steaming jungle houses a profusion of wildlife and exotic vegetation: orangutans and slow loris, flying lizards and hornbills, spectacular fungi, and the garish, evil-smelling rafflesia—a parasitic plant that can produce a flower measuring three feet across and weighing more than 20 pounds. Human settlement is concentrated on the banks of the island's long, wide rivers. While the tangled hinterland is sparsely populated with tribal peoples practicing slash-and-burn agriculture, oil production and logging have given rise to some busy cities near the coast.

2

A house built by the Minangkabau
of western Sumatra bears the rich
decoration and curved gables typical
of Minangkabau architecture. Such
dwellings accommodate extended
families: Grooms move into their
brides' homes, which are enlarged by
extending the walls and adding roofs.

The orchid-shaped island of Sulawesi, formerly known as the Celebes, lies east of Kalimantan and due south of the Philippines, whence Spanish Catholic missionaries set out in the 16th century to convert the natives of the north coast. Reconverted by Dutch Calvinists in the 19th century, the people of this area are among the most Christianized in Indonesia. But Sulawesi's spindly form and steep mountain ranges have cut other inhabitants off from change. Many of the isolated Toraja in the mountain fastnesses have never encountered Islam, let alone Christianity. Their culture is famous for devotion to the dead, which culminates in elaborate funerary feasts.

The Bugis of the southern coast, another ethnic group of Sulawesi, are among the world's most vigorous maritime peoples. Their distinctive gaff-rigged, black- or green-sailed schooners still ply the old sea routes between Sulawesi, Kalimantan, and Java, as they have for centuries past. From 8,000 to 10,000 vessels, each up to 300 long tons deadweight, operate in Indonesian waters—perhaps the largest commercial sailing fleet left in the world. The Bugis' capital, Macassar—now Ujung Pandang—was a center for spice smuggling in the 17th century, before the Dutch monopolized the trade.

The spices were actually grown in the Moluccas, a group of islands to the east of Sulawesi. These remote volcanic specks still produce cloves, nutmeg, and mace; they also have some of the richest fishing grounds in the world. The population is immensely varied. Halmahera, the largest island in the group—but at 6,200 square miles, smaller than New Jersey—is home to more than 30 tribes speaking almost as many languages. Some of the islanders

are Muslims or Christians; still others worship the nature spirits that their distant ancestors revered.

To the south of Sulawesi and the Moluccas, a chain of small, mountainous islands runs east from Java and Bali. Frequent droughts and a scarcity of cultivable level land make this archipelago, collectively known as the Lesser Sundas, one of the poorest island groups in Indonesia. The wildlife, however, is rich and unusual. It includes the Komodo dragon, the world's largest lizard. Reaching 10 feet in length and weighing more than 300 pounds, the "dragons" are swift and powerful enough to prey on wild pigs and deer.

Irian Jaya, the easternmost outpost of Indonesia, is a world unto itself. Its flora and fauna are akin to those of Australia rather than the rest of Asia. Larger than California, Irian Jaya has a population of slightly more than one

million. Protected from the outside world by coastal mangrove swamps and jagged mountains, many of its Melanesian peoples remained Stone-Age hunter-gatherers almost to the present day. They are divided from one another not only by the terrain but by ancient traditions of warfare and headhunting; often a tribe consisting of only a few villages speaks a unique language—unintelligible to outsiders. Although building roads through the formidable mountains is out of the question in the foreseeable future, the people of Irian Jaya are encountering civilization in the shape of schools and medical centers supplied by air.

Irian Jaya's Melanesian peoples are the descendants of the first inhabitants of Indonesia, who arrived some 30,000 years ago. For millennia, they had the archipelago to themselves but were

A statue of the meditating Buddha sits on a terrace atop the 1,200-year-old temple of Borobudur located in central Java. The world's largest Buddhist shrine, Borobudur was buried under volcanic ash for centuries, until it was discovered by an English army colonel in 1814.

eventually joined by mainland Malays who emigrated in two great waves, the first around 3000 B.C., the second about 300 B.C. By the second century B.C., many Indonesians were living in permanent communities, practicing wet-rice agriculture, praying to nature gods, and trading extensively with overseas lands.

A little later, Indonesia began to respond to an influence that would remain powerful for 1,500 years: that of the Indian subcontinent. Successive Indonesian kingdoms employed Brahmin scholars from India and adopted such imports as Buddhism and Hinduism, the Indian script and many Sanskrit loanwords, as well as Indian art and technology. Although Buddhism and Hinduism were eventually overshadowed by Islam, cultural mementos of the period still linger. Bali remains obdurately Hindu, and elsewhere in Indonesia, self-professed Muslims—whose religion will not tolerate idolatry—regularly decorate old Hindu and Buddhist shrines with flowers or similar tokens. And the national emblem of this overwhelmingly Muslim country is the mythical bird called Garuda, the mount of the Hindu god Vishnu.

The earliest great indianized state in Indonesia was Srivijaya, a Buddhist maritime power established in southern Sumatra. From the seventh to the 12th centuries, Srivijaya controlled the lucrative trade through the Strait of Malacca. During that period, a succession of kingdoms sprang up in the fertile rice-growing area of central Java and competed to raise ever more splendid and expensive monuments. The Sailendra dynasty erected the vast Buddhist temple of Borobudur in the eighth century; a few decades later another line, called Mataram, built the equally splendid Hindu temple complex of Prambanan to celebrate a victory over the Sailendras.

In the 10th century, for reasons now obscured by time, the focus in Java shifted to the east. And it was in eastern Java that Majapahit, the most powerful of the early empires, was founded in 1292. It remained a major force for more than a century.

Majapahit could not be described as either a strictly Buddhist or Hindu state, so thoroughly by then had the two religions become fused with each other and with local beliefs, including worship of nature spirits. Majapahit held sway over all Java and Bali; following the collapse of the Srivijaya empire, part of Sumatra became a dependency. According to an account by the court poet Prapanca, the kingdom also received tribute from vassals as distant as Borneo, Sulawesi, and the Moluccas.

Prapanca's accuracy in matters relating to the honor of his ruler, however, is questionable. (He describes a royal dinner at which the king sang "lovable as the call of the peacock sitting in a tree, sweet as a mixture of honey and sugar, touching as the scraping noise of the reeds.") Nevertheless, the empire of Majapahit has offered inspiration for 20th-century nationalist leaders scanning the past for some evidence of Indonesian unity.

Over the centuries, the leisured courtiers of Java's kingdoms developed a philosophy that stressed the need for self-control as the route to spiritual enlightenment. Orderly relationships with others would, they believed, lead to the desired state of inner calm. Etiquette and the art of conversation reached peaks of refinement, and the Javanese language developed its stratified complexity. This philosophy and

A CHRONOLOGY OF KEY EVENTS

c. 3000 B.C. Proto-Malays from the Asian mainland begin migrating to Indonesia, eventually pushing the indigenous Australoid peoples into isolated pockets of the countryside.

c. 100 A.D. Sophisticated kingdoms trading with other parts of Asia are established in Java and Sumatra.

c. 600-1100 The Buddhist kingdom of Srivijaya in south Sumatra controls trade through the Malacca and Sunda straits.

760-820 The Sailendra dynasty builds the great Buddhist monument of Borobudur in central Java.

c. 1250 Arab merchants begin introducing Islam to coastal kingdoms. Over the next few centuries, the religion spreads throughout Indonesia.

1292-1453 The most dominant of the early empires, based at Majapahit in eastern Java, exercises a loose sovereignty over much of Indonesia. Its rulers and people worship the gods and goddesses of the Hindu pantheon (*below*).

1512 The Portuguese reach the Moluccas—the Spice Islands of east Indonesia.

1596 Dutch ships arrive in west Java.

1602 The Dutch East India Company is formed to exploit the highly profitable Eastern spice trade.

1619 The company establishes a base (*above*) at Jakarta, which it renames Batavia. Through conquest and cessions from local rulers, the Dutch come to control most of the island of Java by the end of the 17th century.

1799 Corruption and mismanagement lead to the bankruptcy of the Dutch East India Company. The Dutch government takes over company possessions.

1811-1816 During the Napoleonic Wars, the British capture and govern the Dutch East Indies. In 1816, the Dutch regain control by treaty.

1825-1830 A rebellion known as the Java War threatens Dutch authority. Its leader, Prince Diponegoro, is exiled to Sulawesi.

1830 The Dutch introduce forced cultivation: Peasants must devote a portion of their land to growing export crops for the government.

1870 Permission for Europeans to lease land opens an era of large plantations, especially in Sumatra.

1870-1910 The Dutch impose their rule on the outer islands of Indonesia. Meanwhile, a war against the Aceh sultanate of northern Sumatra ends in victory for the Dutch. Their control of Indonesia is now complete.

1892 Oil starts to flow from wells on the island of Sumatra. By the 1930s, oil is second only to rubber as a source of Indonesia's export income.

1912 Merchants in Java found the Islamic Association, an early channel for radical ideas that develops into a nationalist movement protesting Dutch rule.

1927 The Indonesian Nationalist party is formed under the chairmanship of Sukarno.

1942 The Dutch East Indies fall to the Japanese.

1945 Upon the surrender of the Japanese, Sukarno unilaterally proclaims the independence of the Indonesian republic.

1949 After attempting to reassert control by armed force, the Dutch accept United Nations mediation and grant sovereignty to Indonesia.

1963 Western New Guinea, now known as Irian Jaya, becomes part of Indonesia after the withdrawal of the Dutch.

1965 An attempted coup by junior army officers is blamed on a Communist plot. Government troops and mobs slaughter some 500,000 people, including many Chinese, suspected of being Communist. The army seizes power but retains President Sukarno as a figurehead.

1967 President Sukarno is replaced by General Suharto (*below*).

1975 Indonesia invades and subsequently annexes East Timor, a former Portuguese colony.

1982 Timor elects its first representatives to Parliament.

1987 Preliminary elections held in April reconfirm Suharto.

its social ramifications eventually permeated all of Javanese society. Admiring all that is complex and understated, the Javanese people acquired an aversion to anything coarse or obvious and came to avoid all displays of emotion. These Javanese values have now affected most Indonesians.

The arts that flowered in the early courts were also influenced by the philosophy of restraint. The intricate craft of batik cloth printing, using wax to keep dye from designated areas of the fabric, developed as an occupation for high-born ladies; it was considered a spiritual discipline. Live theater and puppet plays enacted the stories of the Ramayana and the Mahabharata—Indian epics that pivot on the rivalries among semidivine families—but the tales were given moral overtones of the conflict between refined and base feelings. These courtly diversions have long since gained the affection of every level of the population and have spread beyond Java's borders. Batik is worn by practically everyone, and puppet performances still draw villagers who assemble to enjoy the nighttime coolness, smoke Java's distinctly clove-flavored cigarettes, and absorb yet again the moral lessons of the epics.

Marco Polo, the first European traveler to visit Indonesia, reached Sumatra on his way home from China in 1292. At that time, Java's Hindu-Buddhist culture was approaching its golden age, but new currents were already washing the shores of Sumatra. There, Marco Polo encountered many "idolaters," and he noted disapprovingly of one mountain people that "each individual adores throughout the day the first thing that presents itself to his sight when he rises in the morning." But the explorer also discovered that many coastal inhabitants of Sumatra's northern tip were Muslims.

Islam, brought to Indonesian shores by Arab and Gujarati traders, was gradually extending its hold. By the end of the 16th century, most of Java embraced the new faith, as did seaboard peoples of the archipelago's other islands. Small sultanates established on the coasts gradually increased in power; and by the early 15th century, Majapahit was in a state of collapse, rent by conflicts from within and threatened from without.

Although Islam eventually was adopted by 90 percent of Indonesians, those who encountered it reacted in very different ways. The Balinese—for reasons that remain mysterious—rejected it completely. The Javanese, steeped in their courtly traditions, accepted the forms of the religion, such as circumcision, but they retained their pre-Islamic philosophy. On the other hand, the Sundanese people of west Java became ardent Muslims, as did several Sumatran peoples.

In the mid-1980s, about half of Indonesia's Muslims were orthodox, or *santri;* the other half—the *abangan*—were nominal believers and lax often to the point of indifference in applying the laws governing prayer and diet. Abangan beliefs are dominated by Indonesia's indigenous mystical nature worship, blended with Hindu and Buddhist elements. Whereas the *santri* make a point of praying five times a day, learning Arabic, and making at least one pilgrimage to Mecca, the *abangan* do little more than pray on formal occasions.

In 1512, when Islam was continuing to make inroads in Indonesia, another crucial ingredient was added to the cultural mix. Portuguese ships arrived in the archipelago's waters, auguring a European presence that became increasingly dominant over the next 400 years. The newcomers sought cloves and nutmegs—which at that time were found nowhere in the world but the Spice Islands—and fragrant sandalwood, which grew on the Lesser Sundas. Over the next few decades, the Portuguese established trading settlements in the Spice Islands—now the Moluccas—and on Flores and Timor.

The Portuguese soon encountered competition from the Dutch, who founded their East India Company in 1602 to spearhead the struggle for a monopoly of the immensely lucrative spice trade. In 1619, they succeeded in establishing Batavia, now Jakarta, in western Java, and from this permanent headquarters, they expanded their influence, using a combination of force, judicious alliances in local disputes, and treaties with puppet leaders. By the end of the 17th century, they had become the uncontested cultivators and traders in the Spice Islands, though Portugal hung on in the eastern half of Timor until 1975.

Dutch colonial society quickly took on a distinct character of its own. The early officials of the East India Company married local women or lived with Asian concubines. The children of these unions were accepted into the European community, and after the first generation, Dutchmen preferred to marry women of mixed race rather than those of pure Indonesian blood. Men who had contracted mixed marriages often sent their sons back to the Netherlands, but they themselves settled in Java permanently and kept their daughters there to marry the next wave of emigrants. The Dutch retained their

2

A young man marches his family's ducks along a country road in Bali to the flooded rice fields where they will feed. He will stick his long pole into the ground to serve as a beacon for the birds; after gorging on eels and frogs, the ducks will gather around the pole for the waddle home.

wigs and heavy European dress, but many aspects of their new life-style contrasted with the bourgeois routine they had left behind. They spent freely, living in luxury in spacious villas, their wives attended by numerous slaves and diverted with local entertainments such as the shadow play.

For the first half of their long colonial tenure, the Dutch demanded little more than their hold on trade. Fortified bartering stations at river mouths usually marked the extent of their territorial control, and many parts of the archipelago, including much of Java's interior, remained oblivious of the Dutch presence.

Toward the latter part of the 16th century, a second Mataram dynasty had been founded in central Java in the lands of the early Hindu kingdom. The new power was Islamic, but it retained the courtly style of the earlier Javanese kingdoms. In the early 17th century, Mataram conquered most of Java. Its subsequent turbulent history was dominated not only by wars with the Dutch but by heavy fighting among internal factions. In 1755, Mataram's territories were carved in two, and rival rulers established themselves in the neighboring capitals of Jogjakarta and Solo. The Dutch East India Company, having spent a great deal more than it could afford on military entanglements, went bankrupt in 1799.

The Netherlands government took over the company's East Indian possessions immediately, and the independence of Java's feudal princes was doomed. The Dutch stepped up their military presence. The first governor general, Marshall Daendels, treated the princes as vassals and crushed rebellion with force. Meanwhile, Napoleonic France had incorporated the Nether-lands into its empire; in the course of the wars against Napoleon, the British invaded the Dutch East Indies in 1811. For the five years of British rule, Thomas Stamford Raffles, the British lieutenant-governor of Java who later founded Singapore, opposed feudalism and instituted many reforms to favor the peasantry.

In 1816, the archipelago was handed back to the Dutch, who continued the practice started by Daendels and Raffles of intervening at many junctures of native society. High taxes were imposed and discontent grew, eventually exploding into outright war. Between 1825 and 1830, a Javanese Muslim mystic, Prince Diponegoro, led a series of campaigns that cost about 200,000 Javanese and 8,000 European lives.

Diponegoro had become a national hero, but his capture and banishment to Sulawesi was of small comfort to the Dutch, who were in dire economic straits. A solution was sought and found. In 1830, the colonial rulers imposed an infamous policy euphemistically called the Cultivation System, by which every village on Java was obliged to set aside part of its land—at first 20 percent, later 33 percent—to produce export crops—such as coffee, sugar, and indigo—for sale at fixed prices to the government. With the world economy expanding at a terrific rate, the scheme was an unqualified financial success that essentially turned Java into one big Dutch plantation. The peasants, left without enough land to grow their own food, suffered deprivation and sometimes outright starvation.

Meanwhile, the Dutch were steadily extending their control over the outer islands—a process that would be almost complete by 1910. Beginning in 1870, forced cultivation in Java was largely abandoned and colonial attention was diverted to Sumatra, where empty land invited development. Entrepreneurs poured money into the island to develop profitable tobacco, rubber, and sugar plantations. For a while, the Dutch East Indies were the biggest producers of sugar in the world. Toward the end of the century, tin mines and oil fields also came into operation. As a result, Chinese traders, small numbers of whom had been trickling into Indonesia for centuries, began to settle in much larger numbers.

The Dutch population of the Indies increased from 22,000 in 1852 to 75,000 by 1900—most newcomers were planters or entrepreneurs. Women came from the Netherlands in increasing numbers, and as the Dutch became a more self-contained group, the status of those of mixed race fell; they were eventually largely confined to menial jobs in the civil service, where all higher positions were occupied by Dutchmen. As contact with the mother country improved through the telegraph service and faster shipping, many Dutch families in Indonesia felt less constrained than before to cling to European habits unsuited to the climate: They adopted a modified version of Indonesian dress, took midafternoon naps, and ate the local spicy dishes. The adoption of native habits disguised a growing gulf between the rulers and the ruled.

The Dutch in Indonesia spared little concern for the conditions of their subjects. They had no wish to spread education; thousands of Dutch in the Indies were available to fill all the demanding jobs. The abolition of forced cultivation had done little for the Javanese, who still had to pay heavy land taxes. Their population was increasing rapidly and, with the best land already under cultivation, the peasants were finding it increasingly difficult to grow enough food to survive.

It was the populace of the Netherlands rather than the colonialists who, upon hearing reports of appalling conditions among the Indonesians, demanded improvements. The Dutch government responded by investing in agricultural development and transportation, in public health and education. By the early 1930s, one million students were attending school. Technical, law, and medical colleges were founded, and a few talented Indonesians even went to the Netherlands for higher education.

Opportunities for the growing corps of educated Indonesians to shape their country or even their own destinies were limited, however. The Dutch still occupied all administrative posts; Chinese immigrants dominated trade, and industry was practically nonexistent. Educated Indonesians soon focused their energies on nationalism.

One of the early channels for radical ideas was the Islamic Association. Founded in 1912 as an attempt to find a political role for Islam, it attracted a mass membership of both *santri* and *abangan* Indonesians. It was succeeded as a nationalist force by the Communist party, which fomented revolution in the 1920s. The party that was to play a major role in achieving independence was not born until 1927. The Indonesian Nationalist party was founded by a group of graduates led by a 26-year-old engineer named Sukarno (like many Indonesians, he used only one name). He was the man who would proclaim Indonesia's independence in 1945.

Sukarno, who advocated the union of the peoples of the archipelago, had experienced such a bond within his own family. His father was nominally a Muslim Javanese, his mother a Hindu from Bali—a very uncommon match for the period. Sukarno's father was a schoolteacher who instilled in his son the value of a Western education, and who somehow scraped together the money to send him to secondary school and to technical college in Bandung. But Sukarno was also steeped in Java's mystical culture, and to the end of his life, his universe was that of the shadow plays, where endless struggle and conflict achieves a fleeting harmony.

As a schoolboy, Sukarno lodged with Umar Said Tjokroaminoto, the chairman of the Islamic Association, where he imbibed nationalist ideals. As he became politically active, the somewhat shy, withdrawn young man found that

The delicate silhouette of a two-dimensional parchment puppet falls on a screen during a 10-hour performance of a tale from the Hindu Ramayana epic. Often staged with an orchestra, Javanese shadow-puppet theater is one of the most popular performing arts in Indonesia.

he had a gift for oratory. When he graduated as an engineer, he resolved to devote his life to political activism—partly, no doubt, to give vent to the powers he had found within himself, partly because of a genuine concern for his country's plight.

Sukarno made public appearances throughout Java on behalf of the Indonesian Nationalist party, and he wrote many newspaper articles that advocated passive resistance and noncooperation with the Dutch. In 1929, the colonial authorities responded by outlawing the movement and imprisoning Sukarno. Upon his release in 1931, he resumed his activities, spreading the idea of the Indonesian nation and promoting the Indonesian language. In 1933, he was banished to Flores in the Lesser Sundas; he remained in internal exile for 10 years. Peace was restored, and the Dutch planters sipping beer on their verandas took comfort from the statement made by Governor General de Jonge as the dissidents departed: "We have been here for 350 years with stick and sword and will remain here for another 350 years with stick and sword."

But during World War II another power, armed with a bigger stick and a sharper sword, arrived to shatter Dutch dreams. Early in 1942, the Japanese conquered the Dutch East Indies in a matter of weeks. The rout of their colonial masters had a tremendous psychological effect on the Indonesians. Three years of Japanese occupation buoyed their self-confidence and honed their aspirations further. In a bid to mobilize Indonesia in the war effort, the Japanese trained an Indonesian militia that later became the backbone of the Indonesian army. The Japanese also co-opted nationalist leaders such as Sukarno. While purportedly expanding the Japanese cause, the nationalists built up a popular following. With the disappearance of the Dutch into concentration camps, the Indonesians attained high government office for the first time, and Indonesian became the official language.

Although Japanese rule seemed more accommodating than Dutch, disillusionment set in when the occupiers resorted to forced labor and food requisitioning. By late 1944, when it was clear that Japan was losing the war, the only way Japanese leaders could muster faltering Indonesian support was to promise independence. It was with the connivance of the Japanese commander that Sukarno made his independence proclamation, two days after Japan surrendered to the Allies and six weeks before Allied forces, spearheaded by the British, landed to take control of the archipelago.

Soon the Dutch were back. Toward the end of 1945, civilians returned to the major cities of Java and Sumatra, and to many outlying islands. In early 1946, Dutch forces relieved the Allies.

But Dutch supremacy was not so easily restored. In the months after Sukarno's declaration, the euphoria of revolution swept the country. Old scores were settled, and in some places, traditional aristocratic elites were overthrown. Artists and writers produced a spate of powerful works evoking the spirit of the time. Enthusiasm for the new republic was, however, much stronger in Java and Sumatra than elsewhere; in 1946, the Dutch were able to set up an administration in Sulawesi that extended to many outer islands.

The Dutch then began to negotiate with the republican leaders over the possibility of creating a federal system

that would leave the Netherlands in control of large parts of their former possession. The two parties achieved a broad agreement but reached a stalemate over details. In 1947, the Dutch attacked the republican areas of Java and Sumatra in what was described as a "police action." They made some inroads and left the republicans torn by factional rivalries.

Further bloodshed was to follow. In September 1948, the Communist party tried to commandeer the struggle for independence and transform it into a vehicle for general social revolution by attacking republican forces. After two months of bitter fighting Sukarno and his colleagues finally stamped out the rebellion. That threat was hardly over when the Dutch mounted a second "police action." The Indonesians resisted fiercely.

As the guerrilla war continued,

world opinion swung against the colonial power. Under pressure from the United States, which was threatening to withdraw reconstruction aid to the wartorn Netherlands, the Dutch finally agreed to transfer sovereignty. When they did so in 1949, it was in exchange for guarantees safeguarding Dutch investments in Indonesia. Partly for sentimental reasons, the Dutch also insisted on keeping one large possession—western New Guinea.

By the time the Dutch bowed out, Indonesia's leaders had agreed to make their nation a secular state. Sukarno had resisted all suggestions of creating an Islamic republic, which would have alienated the millions of Christians and other minorities, threatening the unity of the country. Indonesia was initially set up as a federal system, but the idea of federation had been discredited in many Indonesians'

47

2

eyes by its association with the departing colonial power; in 1950, a new constitution established a unitary state.

Sukarno was Indonesia's first president, and he remained in power for 20 years. He and his colleagues had to create Indonesia's governing institutions from scratch, since the Dutch, resistant until the end to pleas for independence, had not instituted even a minor degree of self-rule.

Indonesia experimented with a parliamentary system until the late 1950s. A provisional assembly was set up in 1950, and the numerous political parties formed during the independence struggle were granted seats in accordance with their presumed strengths. None had a majority, and quarrelsome, short-lived coalitions became the norm. The Nationalist party that Sukarno had helped found was one of the largest. There were also religious parties, regional parties, and the Communist party—the PKI—which, having recovered rapidly from the odium of the 1948 rebellion, was spreading its membership like wildfire in the countryside. It gained popularity largely by undertaking welfare projects, such as building schools, and in doing so became progressively less radical. The PKI was not, however, offered a place in any of the coalitions. Sukarno allowed the other parties free play but he, as the only constant factor in government, wielded the ultimate power. And he did not hesitate to overturn ministerial decisions when it suited his purpose.

In 1955, elections were finally held, and the number of parties in Parliament increased, instead of shrinking, as most observers had hoped. The coalition that resulted was ineffectual. A number of army officers, disappointed

at the impasse, seized power in Sumatra and some of the other outer islands in 1957. Sukarno imposed martial law to contain the rebellion, and loyal troops reoccupied Sumatra. Martial law gave the military a hold on power that it never relinquished.

Emboldened by his handling of the 1957 crisis, Sukarno became increasingly disenchanted with Parliament: The concept of opposition parties, he felt, was alien to Southeast Asian traditions of consensus. In 1959, he moved to create what he called "Guided Democracy," and Parliament was abolished. Under a changed constitution that gave increased powers to the president, Sukarno created a nonparty cabinet that included army chiefs.

Sukarno rallied immense loyalty as the father of Indonesian independence, and his genius for oratory carried the masses along. The nation accepted his increased powers with equanimity and even enthusiasm. But his move was to bring him new dangers. Previously he had manipulated events behind the scenes without accruing blame; now that he had openly taken a greater share of power, he would suffer in popular esteem from his mistakes.

Although increasingly authoritarian, Sukarno was no dictator: He had to rely on his skill as a manipulator to exert his will against the opposition of other powerful interests—the army, the parties, the regions, and Islam. His charisma and political dexterity were his greatest assets. Because of his popularity, other powerful groups leaned on him for strength, and he became skilled at playing one force against another. The army valued their links with him, and he kept his importunate military allies in check by threatening to bring the Communists into government. The

PKI, with its grass-roots organization, represented a colossal potential power: By the early 1960s, it was the third-largest Communist party in the world in terms of membership, and the world's largest opposition party. Sukarno gave his flirtation with the PKI extra plausibility by establishing cordial relations with Mao's China.

Political surefootedness, however, was no help to Sukarno in handling his most serious problem, the state of the economy. During World War II and the postwar struggle for independence, plantations and mines had been neglected; and exports had plummeted. Peasant farms had suffered too, as a result of the widespread chaos and failure to maintain irrigation systems. Indonesia had been self-sufficient in rice production in 1941, but for many years after the war, it could not even produce enough of the crop to feed its ever-growing population.

President Sukarno failed to tackle the crisis effectively. He talked of instituting land reforms but did little of substance to help the peasants. Large-scale agriculture and mining were badly in need of injections of foreign capital, but Sukarno was stridently hostile to the West, especially to anything that smacked of neo-imperialism. A mass of petty legislation and high taxes discouraged foreign investors. In 1957, Sukarno expelled virtually all of the Dutch nationals in the country and seized numerous foreign estates. Many of the remaining European and American businesses then pulled out of Indonesia, fearing the same fate.

This loss of foreign management skills dealt a serious blow throughout the Indonesian economy. The army took over the running of most of the newly nationalized industries and these

A MOUNTAIN SANCTUARY FOR THE DEAD

Hidden in the mountains of central Sulawesi, the Toraja people lived undisturbed until the arrival of the Dutch in 1905. In their isolation, they developed unique beliefs and customs, most of which centered around death. In the mid-1980s, although some Toraja had converted to Islam or Christianity, many still clung to their ancient funerary rites.

Funerals cost fortunes. To send the deceased into the next world, families may spend all they own on a month-long banquet. To aid the ascent to heaven, the dead are entombed high in a sheer cliff, in holes accessible only by ladders. Lifelike effigies are placed in nearby niches.

Square wooden doors in a limestone burial cliff *(above)* **mark the resting places of Toraja corpses. Ranked effigies of the deceased** *(top)*, **also set into the cliff face, remind the living of the immanence of their ancestors' souls. Out of reverence, the effigies' clothes are regularly changed.**

2

were soon rife with corruption. Inflation rose to around 100 percent per annum between 1961 and 1964.

The president resorted to morale-boosting gestures to demonstrate Indonesia's superiority. In 1955, Indonesia had been the host to representatives of 29 African and Asian nations who met at Bandung in Java—a gathering that would result a few years later in the founding of the Nonaligned Movement. From the time of the Bandung meeting, Sukarno saw it as his mission to turn Indonesia into a world power. Especially in his later years, he traveled the globe in style with a vast entourage. At home, colossal sums were expended on grandiose sports stadiums and monumental statues.

Sukarno also embarked on military adventures. For years, Indonesia had been demanding without success that the Dutch hand over their one remaining possession in the area, western New Guinea. In 1961, matters were brought to a head when Indonesia sent in troops. The Americans, anxious to prevent the oil-rich nation from cutting any more links with the West, put pressure on the Dutch to acquiesce in the invasion. In 1963, they handed over the territory, though not without misgivings, since its small population had few ethnic, cultural, or historical links with distant Jakarta.

The United Nations attempted to win safeguards for the new Indonesians, specifying that the people of the territory, now renamed Irian Jaya, should have a say in their own future. An "Act of Free Choice" was accordingly organized by Jakarta, but not until 1969. Instead of the universal plebiscite envisioned by the United Nations, only 1,022 Irian leaders were consulted. The government succeeded in eliciting the approval of each and every one of them for membership in the nation that had forcibly incorporated their territory six years earlier. But the continuing armed resistance to Indonesian rule indicates that many Irianese are still not reconciled to government from Jakarta.

Sukarno's next diversionary tactic, a confrontation with Malaysia in 1963, was a failure that helped precipitate his own downfall. Violently opposed to British plans to create a federation between newly independent Malaya and the Borneo territories of Sarawak and Sabah, Sukarno tried to destroy this "neo-colonialist conspiracy," first by roughhouse diplomacy, then by sending troops to invade Malaysian Borneo and even to parachute into mainland Malaya. But by 1965, with the army only halfheartedly participating, the campaign reached a stalemate.

While the gloss was wearing off Sukarno's foreign policy, matters were careering out of control on the domestic front. With exports at a virtual standstill, inflation raging at 500 percent, and the price of rice increasing ninefold, the nation was suffering from the effects of Sukarno's reckless economic policies. The Communist party continued to attract supporters; Sukarno had kidney disease and was thought to be near death. Many became convinced that the Communists would shortly insinuate themselves into power. By 1965, Indonesians from all walks of life were unhappy with Sukarno's regime. They included not only members of the armed forces and the business community, but also students and devout Muslims and Christians, all of whom feared an imminent Communist take-over.

Although a coup was expected, the powers in Indonesia found themselves

At a market in the central Balinese village of Ubud, traders under bamboo sunshades display their produce in ample wicker baskets. Among the fruits and vegetables for sale are bananas, chilies, coconuts, mangoes, and sweet potatoes.

2

unprepared when a leftist faction within the army and air force attempted to seize control on the 30th of September, 1965. The conspirators captured and killed 6 out of 7 generals who they alleged were plotting an army insurrection against the president. Missing from the list of victims, however, was General Suharto, commander of the Strategic Reserve, a powerful force whose support was essential if the coup was to be a success.

While President Sukarno vacillated, Suharto took firm steps to foil the attempted coup. He marshaled loyal forces and compelled the rebels to flee to central Java, leaving him in control of Jakarta. Having seized the initiative, Suharto showed no inclination to step out of the limelight.

To what extent the PKI was behind the coup has never been satisfactorily established. Tentative support from Jakarta's leading Communist newspaper on October 2 apparently pointed to at least some involvement, but it seems unlikely that the regional leadership—let alone the rank and file—knew anything of the plot.

Whatever the case, the entire PKI membership was to pay a terrible price. The country slowly succumbed to an orgy of violence, with PKI supporters the main targets, as the army set about eliminating its only real rival. Southeast Asia had known no comparable episode of carnage since World War II. By the time the bloodbath ended in 1966, an estimated half a million Indonesians had been killed, and perhaps twice as many had been imprisoned. In 1977, Amnesty International estimated that as many as 100,000 political prisoners were still held in Indonesia, mainly in penal colonies on the outer islands. By 1980, most had been released.

The onslaught was in part an attack by the army against the left. But it escalated into general unrest and chaos by bringing to light the deep religious and economic antagonisms among Indonesia's people. Sukarno's secular state had angered Indonesia's devout Muslims, many of whom were large landowners who felt personally threatened by Sukarno's promises to carry out land reform. In contrast, most of those who had joined the Communist party were *abangan,* nominal Muslims; politics had added an extra strain to tensions already existing between them and the *santri.*

While the army carried out the massacres in some areas, local Muslim groups, albeit often with weapons supplied by the army, did the killing in most areas. The targets were not just known Communists but ethnic Chinese, who were suspected of having links with mainland China and were regarded as outsiders.

Sukarno could do nothing to halt the terror. After the attempted coup, he tried to act as though authority were still in his hands, but discovered that Suharto was now the effective leader of the country. Suharto did not bother to challenge Sukarno's official pronouncements; he merely paid no attention to them and issued his own edicts. Frequently, Sukarno was forced into embarrassing retractions.

The military leaders were in no hurry to strip Sukarno of the trappings of power. They knew that he was still a hero to many Indonesians. And although many other people approved of tying Sukarno's hands, they were not yet ready to trust Suharto. But after an unsuccesful attempt by Sukarno in February 1966 to assert his authority in a controversial cabinet reshuffle, the

army formally forced him to delegate supreme authority to General Suharto. For another year, Sukarno remained president. He spoke in public as if he were still the man who decided Indonesia's fate, but his views were ignored and his former policies overturned. In 1967, the provisional military government finally felt strong enough to relieve him of his office and name Suharto as the acting president. Sukarno died in 1970, but his regime—known today in Indonesia as the "Old Order"—had passed away with the attempted coup of 1965.

Pragmatic, cautious, and private, Suharto was the antithesis of his volatile and populist predecessor. The son of a landless peasant, he was born in 1921 in central Java and spent his boyhood within a day's journey of the courts of Jogjakarta and Solo. He entered the Dutch East Indian Army at the age of 18 and rose rapidly in its ranks. During the 1945-1949 war against the Dutch, he led guerrilla troops; after the transfer of sovereignty, he remained a professional soldier, reaching the rank of major-general by 1962. Suharto was universally admired as a brave and astute soldier, but until the 1965 attempted coup, he appeared to have little interest in government. He soon revealed himself, however, as a brilliant politician whose judgment and timing could rarely be faulted.

While Sukarno's overriding aim had been to foster the idea of the Indonesian nation and its greatness, Suharto was able to take nationhood and unity as a given and concentrate on more concrete matters. Hence many of the policies of Suharto's "New Order" took Indonesia in radical departures from Sukarno's line. In the foreign field, Su-

Schooners, built and sailed by the Bugis people of Sulawesi, lie moored by a quay in Jakarta after delivering lumber from Borneo. The Bugis are renowned seafarers who still ply the extensive trader networks connecting Indonesia's many islands.

harto retained affectionate links with the Nonaligned Movement—but he severed the bonds that Sukarno had forged with China and turned instead toward the non-Communist countries, particularly the United States and Japan, for economic aid. Suharto even buried the hatchet with Malaysia, formally establishing links with Indonesia's former enemy in 1967, the year ASEAN was created.

Only once in the first 20 years of his military administration did he involve Indonesia in a foreign adventure of the kind Sukarno undertook in Irian Jaya. Suharto's goal was the former Portuguese colony of East Timor. The colonial forces had fled their possession in 1975 after one of East Timor's three main political parties seized power. But after a brief civil war it was another party, the leftist Revolutionary Front of Independent East Timor (Fretelin),

that gained control. The specter of a Cuba in Indonesia's midst proved too much for Suharto's anti-Communist temper. In December, Indonesian troops invaded East Timor, and it became a province of Indonesia in 1976. Fretelin, however, went into the rugged, brush-covered hills to wage guerrilla war. Ten years later, the fighting was still going on, having claimed the lives of about 10 percent of the island's 200,000 inhabitants.

Elsewhere in the country, though, the first 20 years of Suharto's New Order were relatively calm. To an extent, the stability was imposed by force rather than by consent. From the start, Suharto controlled the two institutions that matter in Indonesia—the army and the civil service. Freedoms have remained much narrower than they were even under Sukarno. But among the peasantry, opposition has in any case

been muted by memories of the traumatic 1965 bloodbath, while both peasants and the influential middle class have benefited from the prosperity generated by the New Order.

Suharto reversed Sukarno's policy toward foreign investors who, after a period of skepticism, once more flocked in, attracted by Indonesia's range of natural resources, especially its low-sulfur crude oil. The oil was found in 1883, when a Dutch planter in north Sumatra noticed a torch burning in a cabin. When he asked what fueled the flame, his host showed him a nearby spring covered with a thick, tarry skin. That chance discovery led to the formation of the Royal Dutch Shell Company, which still has residual interests in Indonesia. But, today, oil production is under the overall control of Pertamina, the state oil and gas company set up during the Sukarno era.

2

Flare stacks burn off excess gas at an oil-drilling installation in the swampy delta of the Mahakam River in east Kalimantan. Indonesia produces 2 percent of the world's oil, enough to satisfy 75 percent of its domestic energy needs and bring in two thirds of its foreign-exchange earnings.

Flare stacks burn off excess gas at an oil-drilling installation in the swampy delta of the Mahakam River in east Kalimantan. Indonesia produces 2 percent of the world's oil, enough to satisfy 75 percent of its domestic energy needs and bring in two thirds of its foreign-exchange earnings.

Indonesia's oil, which it can sell at a premium over most other grades, has been both boon and burden: the key to the country's economic progress, but also an easy corrupter and a spawner of grandiose visions. During the 1970s and early 1980s, it dominated all other resources, bringing in 70 percent of total export receipts. In the late 1980s, 70 percent of Indonesia's oil came from Sumatra, 20 percent from Kalimantan, and 5 percent from Irian Jaya. Produc-

tion was falling as reserves shrank, but Pertamina had diversified into natural-gas production. It was the largest exporter of liquefied natural gas in the world; Japan and South Korea are its largest markets.

The oil windfall and better economic management allowed Suharto to tackle many development problems that defeated Sukarno. Between 1972 and 1978, for example, over 25,000 primary schools were built, and the num-

ber of doctors increased fivefold.

Oil money was also being poured into industrial projects. In the 1970s, Indonesia concentrated on developing labor-intensive industries, such as plywood and batik-cloth printing. Now the emphasis has shifted to engineering, electronics, and oil-derived products such as fertilizer. The nation manufactures automotive parts under license and makes airplanes in a joint venture with Spanish businesses. Because it has

Children congregate around the attendant at a rudimentary gas station in southern Sumatra. The gas cans arrayed at the front of the booth contain locally extracted crude oil, diesel fuel, kerosene for stoves and lamps, and gas for the motorcycles owned by 1 in 30 Indonesians.

a burgeoning work force and low rates of pay, Indonesia has an edge as an exporter over regional competitors such as Malaysia or even Thailand. But growing Western protectionism has hindered the country in its efforts to boost its nonoil exports.

Agriculture, like manufacturing, benefited from the easy oil money. As recently as 1977, Indonesia had to import one third of the world's surplus rice to feed its population. In 1984, however, it became a rice exporter for the first time in more than 40 years. The turnaround came as a result of new irrigation projects, the introduction of pest-resistant rice strains, larger storage capacity, and increased credit for rice farmers. The attainment of self-sufficiency in a society that equates rice with prosperity has been a source of great pride.

In the early 1980s, when Indonesia finally began to concern itself seriously with what its prospects would be when the oil ran dry, even the long-neglected plantation sector started to attract attention. By the mid-1980s, the area devoted to plantations—chiefly of sugar cane, rubber trees, and oil palms—was growing at the rate of nearly 2.5 million acres annually. The majority of these new undertakings were in Kalimantan and Sumatra.

The military has been deeply involved in every move to develop Indonesia's resources. Indeed, seeing itself both as a source of stability and a force that can propel the country into prosperity, the army lays claim to a permanent role in the direction of all civilian life. Its major role in business started with the seizure of Dutch assets under Sukarno. Since then, the lines between the armed forces, government, and industry have become ever more blurred.

During the first two decades of the New Order, hundreds of pensioned-off generals were granted nominal directorships on the boards of government corporations. After 1982, Indonesia's president and vice president were retired generals, as was one third of the cabinet, and one quarter of the seats in the Dewen Perwakilan Rakyat, the country's largely ceremonial Parliament, were reserved for retired generals. At every level of government—provincial, district, and subdistrict—the armed forces' reach is evident; even Indonesia's village chiefs are often retired sergeants.

The other ubiquitous fact of Indonesian public life is corruption. It augments civil servants' meager wages, speeds up business applications, and helps traders avoid the full weight of their annual tax burdens. At these petty levels, most Indonesians resignedly accept unscrupulous behavior as virtually the only force that keeps the ponderous bureaucracy going. But they resent the large-scale venality that has brought wealth to those at the apex of Indonesian society. Some efforts have been made to clean up the system. The ports, for example, used to be so notorious for devious practices that in 1985, President Suharto took the unexpected step of pensioning off his entire customs service, and he even went so far as to put a Swiss contractor on the docks to assess duties.

Complex and deeply compromising links exist between senior army personnel and merchants. Many of the latter are Chinese Indonesians, who still occupy the highest-level jobs in the economy. Most of the suspect business ties were cemented during the first days of independence, when divisional army commanders—among them Su-

Palm trees fringing a sandy shore in southeast Bali highlight the tropical beauty that has made the isle Indonesia's prime tourist attraction. Most visitors are drawn to the coast, which offers superb beaches and coral reefs, surfing, and skin diving.

harto himself—coped with inadequate funding from Jakarta by teaming up with non-native Indonesians to create their own businesses. The purpose was ostensibly to supply and feed their troops, but immense personal fortunes often accrued along the way. To this day, the Chinese pay extortionate amounts of protection money to their associates in the armed forces.

Indonesians who are unhappy with the way the army is running their country have few legitimate outlets for their complaints. The broadcasting networks are government-owned and controlled; the print media, fearful of any government interference, exercises severe self-censorship and addresses controversial subjects only by innuendo and analogy. Golkar, Indonesia's main political party under Suharto, is controlled by the military. Government pressure on the electorate has ensured that Golkar receives a large percentage of the vote in every general election. The left was wiped out in the pogrom of 1965, and the Communist party has been outlawed since 1966.

In the opposition vacuum, the country's Muslim community has become the main channel of protest. A radical minority, deeply influenced by the worldwide Islamic political resurgence of the 1980s, the Muslims have been critical of the administration's obsession with development and offended by a perceived indifference to Islam's strictures by senior members of the government.

The government, correctly viewing the Muslim right as its one remaining political threat, has endeavored to eliminate ideology from politics. The official state philosophy, called Pancasila—five principles—is a program calling for belief in God, humanitarianism, na-

tional unity based on consensus and representation, and social justice. Conspicuously absent from the list of objectives is any mention of a specific religion. In addition, the government has consistently made life difficult for religious zealots. In 1972, it forced four Islamic parties to merge as the United Development party (PPP). The PPP leaders forged ties with the government, which gave them at least a hearing, but their effectiveness was steadily eroded by internal rifts and by government decrees, including one that forbade them to use the holy Kaaba stone in Mecca as their symbol.

Deprived of an influential voice in national politics, radical Islam began expressing itself in violence. An unruly mosque meeting in Jakarta in 1984 was followed by a spate of bomb and arson attacks on Chinese businessmen, a Catholic seminary, and the Buddhist monument of Borobudur. The government acted quickly and uncompromisingly; troops sent in to crush the riot in Jakarta fired on the crowd and killed at least 40 people.

Despite such rumblings of discontent, there is a feeling among most Indonesians that their country has come of age after two decades of frenetic nation building under Sukarno and another two decades of more tangible achievement under Suharto. In this respect the country's 40th anniversary, celebrated with a month-long round of military parades and cultural events in 1985, had a special significance. In Java's complex culture, people measure their lives by cyclical five-year periods called *windus,* and a person with eight *windus* behind him is believed to have entered the mature and fulfilling period of life. As for a man or woman, so also for a nation. □

ANCIENT TRADITIONS OF A JAVANESE COURT

The royal city of Jogjakarta, a survivor from the island's monarchic past, is still Java's cultural hub. The city was founded in 1755 after a power struggle within the ruling Mataram dynasty, which continued to garner respect and influence even while the Dutch were extending their control over Java. Prominent in the 20th-century struggle against Dutch rule, the sultan of Jogjakarta was made governor of the city and surrounding province after independence, retaining much of his ancestors' temporal authority.

Jogjakarta inherited and refined the elaborate artistic culture developed in earlier Javanese kingdoms. The dance, theater, music, architecture, and handicrafts patronized by the court drew on a rich fusion of native Indonesian, Buddhist, and Hindu influences. But the rulers of Jogjakarta were Muslim, and the city's greatest displays were on Islamic feast days. Today, the sultan's family still fosters Java's courtly arts and celebrates the high points in the Muslim calendar with the pomp of former times.

Accompanied by courtiers, a son of Jogjakarta's sultan officiates at a Muslim festival held in the palace. The gold umbrella is the prerogative of royalty; other colors were once associated with different ranks in the Javanese social hierarchy.

Serpents and a giant's head adorn a rail around the palace ballroom. The images represent numbers—snakes, the guardians of the eight winds, signify eight. Together the carvings show the date the ballroom was built: 1853 in Javanese chronology, equivalent to 1923 A.D.

One of the sultan's corps of cleaners dusts the teak pillars and porcelain pots that surround the Golden Pavilion, the innermost reception and ceremonial area of the palace.

The palace at the heart of the city of Jogjakarta dates back to the 18th century; within its encircling walls are quarters for the sultan's extensive family, ornate state rooms, and spacious open-sided pavilions. Retainers care for the buildings and their inmates.

The palace was once the core of a more extensive complex that included a mosque, markets, parade grounds, and royal pleasure gardens. These outer structures are no longer part of the palace proper, but many of the houses beyond the inner enclave are still owned and occupied by relatives of the sultan.

Ladies-in-waiting carrying tea to the sultan's wives file through a courtyard.

A court attendant rests in the shade of a pavilion after completing his daily tasks; out of respect, he faces the sultan's residence.

THE NOBLE ART OF DANCE

In Jogjakarta's heyday, dance was one of the most assiduously cultivated arts. The leading roles were generally reserved for aristocrats, although members of the lower orders took supporting parts. The first classical dance school beyond the palace walls was not created until 1918. In the late 1980s, Jogjakarta had about 20 dance companies, and performances both inside and outside the palace set the standard for the country.

Many of the dances dramatize stories from two Indian epics, the Ramayana and the Mahabharata.

While a chorus and soloists sing an accompaniment, the performers move through a series of angular yet fluid positions, using subtle hand gestures to suggest emotion. Performances within the palace are choreographed according to tradition, but some of the outside companies experiment with new styles.

Dances are accompanied by the traditional Javanese gamelan orchestra of up to 30 instruments, mostly percussive. The drums, xylophones, and many gongs create a complex, shimmering texture of sound.

Flanked by other members of a gamelan orchestra, a musician plays brass gongs.

Two Javanese dancers enact in stylized movement an episode from the Ramayana in which the hero, Rama *(right)*, draws comfort from his younger brother, Lesmana. Both men wear one of the traditional batiks of the Jogjakarta court draped over their patterned trousers. Their armbands, necklets, wings, and headgear are made of leather and painted gold.

REVIVING PAST PAGEANTRY

On the Islamic feast day of Garebeg Besar, the citizens of Jogjakarta take part in lively celebrations that combine religion with the traditions of old court life. In a procession headed by the sultan or one of his sons, huge offerings of rice, vegetables, and sweets are carried from the palace to the mosque in the city's main square. At the mosque, the food is then distributed to the crowd. Everyone tries to obtain a share of the offering to ensure well-being as well as to guard against bad luck.

In the past, the sultan's parade was accompanied by 800 palace guards. The sultan's retinue was disbanded during World War II, however, and has been replaced by a corps of civilian volunteers.

Residents of Jogjakarta, wearing traditional batik sarongs and blue shirts, parade through the streets in rehearsal for the Garebeg Besar procession. On the day of the festival, the marchers will don the military costumes of the old palace guard.

The hilt of an Indonesian dagger juts from the belt of a marcher; his brass pouch bears the sultan's crest.

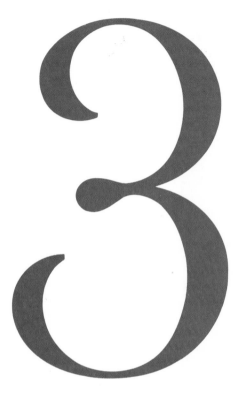

Silhouetted against Kuala Lumpur's city hall and a colonial clock tower, the domes and minarets of the Jame Mosque are a symbol of identity to Malaysia's largest native ethnic group. Allegiance to Islam is one feature that distinguishes the politically dominant Malays.

A PARTNERSHIP OF CULTURES

Between the two limbs of Malaysia's territory lie 440 miles of tropical sea, giving the country an oddly dislocated appearance on the map. On the ground, though, West Malaysia—the peninsula descending southward from Thailand—bears a resemblance to East Malaysia, which comprises the states of Sarawak and Sabah in northern Borneo. In both halves of the nation, the land slopes gently up from mangrove swamps at the sea's edge and then rises abruptly to a mountainous spine. In both halves, too, jungle is abundant: Despite extensive logging operations in recent years, rain forests still covered more than 70 percent of the land during the late 1980s—a higher proportion than in any other Southeast Asian country, with the exception of Brunei.

The rain forests of eastern Malaysia, however, are far more extensive than those of western Malaysia: In fact, the Malaysian and Indonesian sections of Borneo together make up the largest tract of untouched rain forest in the whole of Southeast Asia. All the towns of any importance in Sarawak and Sabah are strung along the coast; neither roads nor railways slice a path through the forested interior.

In West Malaysia, unbroken rain forest is confined to the central mountain ridge. On lower ground, stretches of jungle are interspersed with villages surrounded by rice fields, with plantations of regimented rubber trees and oil palms, and with dynamic modern

cities. The contrast between the primeval bush in the Pahang hills and the glass towers of nearby Kuala Lumpur is as stark as any in Asia. Cobras occasionally slither into lush suburban gardens; elephants are now rare south of the Thai border, but tigers still roam parts of the countryside.

The wilderness encroaches because the people are few: Malaysians number only 16 million. Sabah and Sarawak, in particular, are sparsely settled. Throughout Malaysia, however, the population makes up in complexity what it lacks in numbers.

The main indigenous inhabitants of peninsular Malaysia are the Malays: farmers and fishermen descended from migrants who arrived from mainland Asia around 300 B.C. In Sarawak and Sabah, there are tribal peoples whose ancestors arrived in this part of the world from the Asian hinterland even earlier than the forebears of the Malays. The Iban, whose warlike ancestors were headhunters, are the most numerous ethnic group in Sarawak; they cultivate rice by the slash-and-burn method. The Kadazans, historically a more pacific people, predominate in Sabah.

In addition to its various indigenous groups, Malaysia also accommodates Chinese and Indian populations large enough to make the Malays a minority in their native land: They make up just 47 percent of the population. The Malays are also part of a larger group

3

A vendor of Chinese noodle soup pedals his cart to a busy street corner in Penang. Other entrepreneurs serve such foods as Malay-style skewered chicken or Indian pancakes. Malaysians are addicted to snacks, and they willingly sample the specialities of different culinary traditions.

known as *bumiputras*—indigenous peoples such as the Iban and the Kadazan. Altogether these so-called Sons of the Soil constitute 59 percent of Malaysia's population. Chinese account for 32 percent of the population and Indians 8 percent. Engendering both rich diversity and occasional bitter division, Malaysia's ethnic complexity affects all aspects of social, economic, and political life in the country today.

The Chinese and Indians are found in cities nationwide—in East Malaysia as well as West Malaysia—and in some parts of the countryside, too. They are especially well represented along the densely populated western flank of the peninsula. Indeed, these small towns, whose inhabitants come from diverse ethnic backgrounds, are microcosms of the entire nation.

One such community is Rantau, a little town near mainland Malaysia's western coast. Terraces of two-story, open-fronted, tile-roofed dwellings stand on either side of the highway that serves as Rantau's main street. Upstairs in these "shophouses"—the combined homes and workplaces of the Chinese—children sit from dawn to dusk watching Cantonese or Hokkien dialect videotapes—a steady diet of Hong Kong soap operas that will sustain them until they reach the age of seven and go to school. On the ground floor, their fathers, dressed in white shirts and shorts, run general stores and restaurants and modest wholesale businesses. In the street, Chinese chefs fry noodles at outdoor stalls and take orders from passing truck drivers who have stopped for refreshment.

Just beyond the Chinese dwellings are the carved-wood stilt houses of the Malays. Outside the houses, sarong-clad peasants tend flowers and fruit trees in spacious gardens that overlook irrigated rice fields and, perhaps, a few rows of rubber trees. Malay men gossip animatedly in the nearby coffeehouse; their wives gather to chat on the verandas in front of some of the houses. The mosque where the Malays congregate to worship every Friday stands on the outskirts of town; scattered among the homes are chapel-size prayerhouses where the pious repair to pray five times a day.

The small farms of the Malay adjoin large company-run palm-oil and rubber plantations. Beyond the town, past the police station, fruit market, and bus depot, are the plantation headquarters and the cramped compounds of the Indians who are employed to tap the rubber trees and harvest the fruit of the oil palms. Lines of men and sari-clad women labor together in the dappled shade of the leaves. A brightly painted temple that is dedicated to the Hindu lord Subrahmanya can be seen between the rows of trees.

The division of occupations exemplified by Rantau goes back to imperial times, when the British—anxious not to disturb traditional local society—left the Malays in their rural settings and encouraged rootless immigrants to develop modern sectors of the economy. But since independence, strong economic growth coupled with preferential treatment of indigenous peoples have helped dissolve the colonial-era rigidities. The world's largest producer of tin, rubber, and palm oil, Malaysia has also become a manufacturer and a major oil producer. Increasing numbers of *bumiputras* are heading for the cities in search of government-funded university scholarships and jobs at all levels of industry.

Nowhere are the new wealth and the

Members of Malacca's Chinese community make offerings to their gods and ancestors in the city's Cheng Hoon Teng Temple. Although Islam is the state religion of Malaysia, the constitution guarantees freedom of worship to its non-Malay citizens.

new middle class more obvious than in Kuala Lumpur. The capital and its environs are home to more than one million people—1 out of 14 is Malaysian. Yet only a century ago the area was a collection of Chinese tin-miners' shacks located at the highest navigable point of the silt-laden Kelang River, which gave the city its name: "muddy estuary."

Some of Kuala Lumpur's wealthier suburbs are reminiscent of the colonial heyday earlier this century: villas set among orchids and hibiscus that provide oases of green tranquillity. But much of the charm that once lured British expatriate bureaucrats back to "KL" for second and third tours of duty has vanished in the last few years of hectic growth.

The mock-Moghul clock tower that dominates the main 19th-century administration building now seems di-minutive in comparison with the soaring headquarters of Malaysia's new corporations, many crowned with a helipad. Ministerial offices have been shifted from prefabricated, two-story buildings to a hexagonal, 45-story skyscraper with a gleaming white-tiled exterior and a brown marble interior. An expensive reorganization of main boulevards begun in the 1970s was completed in the mid-1980s, just in time to be overwhelmed by the increase in traffic caused by the mania for private cars that afflicts every self-respecting aspirant to the middle class.

In the past, the different ethnic groups occupied distinct areas of the city. But the government has made a deliberate attempt to break the pattern in the new housing developments that have sprung up on former rubber plantations. The middle-level managers and the skilled workers of all cultures who have moved in have become accustomed to living cheek by jowl with their counterparts from other ethnic backgrounds. And the downtown Selangor Club, where generations of white planters sipped their gin, has become a congenial watering hole for the new political and business elite of every creed and color.

Kuala Lumpur's new wealth is founded upon a centuries-old tradition of trade. Soon after settling on the peninsula around 300 B.C., the Malays began to exploit their position on the sea route between China and the West. By about 100 A.D., they had established trading links with India and China.

Absorbing cultural influences from India in particular, communities on the peninsula coalesced over the centuries

3

into small Hindu or Buddhist states. In the 15th century, one of these states rose to preeminence in the region. Its name was Malacca, and it had the good fortune to be located at the narrowest point on the Strait of Malacca, one of the world's most heavily traveled waterways, as well as to be ruled by a succession of strong princes. It became a great trading center, renowned as an entrepôt for pepper, edible birds' nests, tortoise shells, camphor, pearls, gold, and tin. Its court became a legend for wealth and opulence.

After a succession struggle in 1444, Muzaffar Shah, a zealous adherent to Islam, ascended the throne and made Malacca a Muslim state. He adopted the title of sultan, and his successors fol-lowed suit. Islamic elements were interpolated into the elaborate court pageantry inherited from the Hindu-Buddhist period. Previously, Islam had reached only isolated spots on the peninsula, but thereafter conversion was rapid. Malacca's religious influence spread as far as Borneo through trade and matrimonial links: The king of Brunei, who maintained loose control over the northern coast of the island, became a convert and began to style himself sultan.

At the beginning of the 16th century, when Malacca was at the height of its power, it ruled much of the Malay Peninsula and part of Sumatra. Its golden age lasted little more than a century, however. Portugal seized the capital in 1511, and the sultan fled. But the Portuguese wanted Malacca only as a trading post, and they made no attempt to penetrate the interior. And neither did the Dutch, who took Malacca from Portugal in 1641. Meanwhile, the Malaccan aristocracy founded new dynasties elsewhere on the peninsula and re-created the pomp of the old court.

More than a century elapsed between the Dutch seizure of Malacca and the arrival of the colonial power that was to have the greatest impact on Malaysia. In 1786, the British took their first bite of the country, securing the island of Penang from a local sultan; in 1824, the Dutch ceded Malacca to Britain. Beginning in 1826, Penang, Malacca, and Singapore were administered as a sin-

A VILLAGE UNDER ONE ROOF

The Iban, the most populous ethnic group in Sarawak, recall a turbulent past when every community was at war with its neighbors. Faced with the constant threat of raids, as many as 70 families lived together in shared homes more than 850 feet long. Raised on stilts for extra protection, the houses were usually built on the banks of rivers, which provided water, food, and easy access by canoe.

Today peace reigns, and some Ibans now take jobs in the state's fast-growing coastal oil towns. Most, though, still practice shifting cultivation in the forested interior and choose to live in longhouses. Inside the bamboo-and-thatch structures, separate families occupy individual rooms articulated by a wide corridor running the length of the building—an arrangement that permits some privacy in a highly public life-style.

A longhouse faces the Rejang River, its only link with the outside world.

gle unit, the "Straits Settlements." The resulting administrative stability encouraged Chinese and Indian traders to set up shop in Penang and Malacca. These early settlers, especially the Chinese, integrated themselves into local life. Although they retained their own religious rites, they learned to speak Malay and cook Malayan food.

Later generations of immigrants were not so easily assimilated. From the mid-19th century onward, Chinese, forced to leave their homeland by revolution, flood, or famine, immigrated in order to exploit Malaysia's tin resources. The West had imported modest amounts of this metal for centuries, but the industrial revolution, by stimulating demand for an inert coating that protected against corrosion, greatly expanded the market. Tin-plated steel cans for food became commonplace. The Malays lacked the capital and skills to intensify the mining operations; instead, sultans leased land to immigrants from China who organized work gangs of their compatriots to dig up the metal.

The Malays thought of the newcomers as temporary residents, and the Chinese themselves concurred. They retained their own customs and stayed out of local politics. Coming from many different regions of southern China and speaking numerous dialects, they were more concerned with conflicts in their own community. The rivalries grew so bitter and intense that the years between 1855 and 1875 are remembered in Malaysia as the era of the "Wars of the Chinese Miners." The strife had its origins in gambling quarrels, which in turn led to murders. Revenge killings sparked battles between rival Chinese secret societies, driving thousands of Chinese from one sultanate to another.

The disorder caused by the feuding eased the way for the imposition of British rule over the peninsula. In the early 1870s, the anarchy was disrupting tin exports; Chinese and European middlemen in the Straits Settlements called upon the British government to reestablish law and order. In 1874, the imperial power effected a treaty with a pretender to the sultanate of Perak,

Men repair fishing nets and dogs snooze in the shared section of the longhouse. The door to one family's private area is on the right.

3

marking a new phase in colonial history. In exchange for British recognition and support, the sultan accepted a British Resident, who in theory had no executive powers but in fact quickly established himself as the de facto ruler. In subsequent years, three other sultanates in the middle of the Malay Peninsula were similarly co-opted into the British Empire.

In 1896, a federal government for the Federated Malay States—as the four sultanates had become known—was established in Kuala Lumpur. The sultans retained the trappings of authority, but real power had been discreetly removed. The five remaining sultanates on the peninsula resisted being incorporated into the federation. All of them, however, came under considerable British control at the end of the 19th century.

Well before any of the mainland sultanates had acquiesced to the British, the escapades of an English adventurer caused part of the sultan of Brunei's territory to pass into British hands. James Brooke, the son of a wealthy employee of the East India Company, was born in India and served as a military officer there until he was 35. But then, craving a more glorious destiny, he set sail in his own ship for Sarawak. He found the province in a state of anarchy, its various tribes at war with one another and piracy rife along the coast. Brooke used his schooner to reduce piracy and his charisma to win over the various native factions. Before long, he had established his authority as the only man capable of keeping control in the area. In 1841, the sultan's uncle, the governor of Sarawak, recognized Brooke's services by installing him as Sarawak's ruler. He remained raja until his death in 1868, when his nephew—

Variations on the traditional stilt house manifest the pride that Malays take in immaculate homes and well-tended gardens. These spacious structures belong to the well-to-do; most people live in one-story dwellings.

later followed by his grandnephew—succeeded to the throne of the "white rajas." The unlikely dynasty endured for a century.

In the meantime, North Borneo—the area known today as Sabah—had also entered the British sphere of influence. It was leased from the sultan of Brunei by an enterprise called the British North Borneo Company, which in 1881 was granted a royal charter. The company made a modest profit by cultivating tobacco and by exporting birds' nests for Chinese soup. It was supposed to administer and develop the territory internally while leaving foreign relations to the British government. In practice, however, neither the British North Borneo Company nor the government interfered much in the affairs of this underpopulated backwater, although British missionaries did spread Christianity among the tribal peoples in the area.

The Malay Peninsula, in contrast, was profoundly affected by the British: Britain's endeavors encouraged immigration, which has led to deep divisions in the country. British entrepreneurs modernized tin extraction, replacing labor-intensive pit mines with alluvial dredges that turned great tracts of the peninsula into moonscapes. The British also provided the infrastructure to shift the metal, cutting roads and railways through the mountains and building bridges across fast-flowing rivers. The tin industry multiplied in size, and in response to the demand for miners, the Chinese population—roughly 150,000 in 1874—grew to more than two million by 1911.

The Chinese were not destined to remain tin miners for long. Endowed with enterprise and drive, many of them were busy carving themselves a firm niche in real estate, manufacturing, and moneylending by the beginning of this century. Some became extremely rich and inevitably excited the envy of the Malays. Yet the Chinese, sundered by dialect and clan, lacked a common voice that would help them gain political influence. They were unanimous only in refusing to be assimilated. The Islam of the native Malays posed a formidable barrier to social intercourse, and in any case, the Chinese still thought of mainland China as a home to which they expected to return when they had earned enough money to buy a parcel of land or to establish a business.

While the Chinese made their fortunes in Malaysia's towns, the British were embarking on a new venture in the countryside—turning the jungle-clad slopes into a parade ground of rubber trees. Progress was slow at first, but after the turn of the century the use of rubber for tires on motor vehicles caused demand to soar. The golden years were from 1900 to 1930. Even today, with other commodities gradually replacing rubber, Malaysia has five million acres of the crop, 60 percent of all West Malaysia's cultivated land, and almost two million people depend on it for their livelihood.

Most of the British planters, like the civil servants who administered the protectorate, saw Malaya as only a temporary home. In contrast to the Dutch settlers in Indonesia, many of whom had been there for generations, the British came to make their careers in their twenties and retired to England in their sixties. During their sojourn in Malaya they worked hard, drank freely, and congregated in the local European clubs to play bridge and browse through yellowing newspapers.

The workers—who quickly became skilled at the delicate but tedious task of tapping rubber trees for latex—were for the most part impoverished Tamils imported in contract gangs from Madras. These Indians, confined to the rubber plantations by their brutal coolie foremen, lived in cramped, disease-ridden row tenements, and died in the remote malaria-infested jungle.

Other Indians came to the towns and cities of Malaya to run the railroads,

3

open candy stores, and teach in the schools. Some of their children bettered themselves and became lawyers and doctors. Although they were less isolated than the workers who were locked away on the plantations, the urban Indians remained outside the Malayan mainstream. An intricate structure of snobbery reinforced religious and caste prejudice.

Like the Chinese and Indians, the Malays themselves were a mixed group. The ethnic makeup of the indigenous population had been altered by Arab and Indian Muslim traders, by Thai and Borneo bloodlines, and also by 20th-century migrants from Indonesia. The traditional designation of Malays as *bumiputras* became a rough approximation when so many of the Malays were first-generation immigrants from thousands of miles away. As genealogy became less significant in the definition of a Malay, three other factors grew in importance: the Malay language, the religion of Islam, and devotion to the nine sultans.

The British, far more than the Dutch in Indonesia, were careful to support the Malays, not only in cultivating the favors of the native aristocracy but in protecting Islam from outside influences. British Residents were often well-versed in local languages and customs. Some Malays received a Western-style education and secured low-level jobs in the civil service. The Chinese and Indians, in contrast, were kept out of the administration. Using such patronage as evidence, the British laid claim to being the one force that protected Malay integrity in the face of the flood of immigrants. Malays at every level of society accepted this claim and did not later turn against the sultans for collaborating with the colonial power.

A bus winds its way through a tea plantation in the Cameron Highlands—a tract of forested hills in the center of West Malaysia. The Highlands are popular with tourists, who are drawn by the temperate climate and panoramic views.

When independence was granted, the Malay people were economically weak in comparison with the Chinese, but they were stronger politically, thanks to the rallying power of their religion and their rulers.

There was little call for independence in the early decades of the 20th century; it took World War II to sharpen aspirations. The war began for Malaysia late in 1941, when Japanese invaders swept through the ill-defended country in 55 days. Sarawak and North Borneo fell to Japan in February of 1942. About 70,000 military and civilian British were captured and interned, most of them in Singapore.

During their four-year occupation, the Japanese treated Malaysians in markedly different ways depending on their ethnic background. The new masters were conciliatory toward the Indians, who they hoped would join Japanese-sponsored anti-British armies. With the Malays, the policy was more ambiguous: Discipline was strict, but the position of the sultans was left undisturbed. The real victims of the invasion were the Chinese, who were treated savagely.

Eventually, the cruelty of the occupation forces, the hunger and deprivation experienced by all ethnic groups, and the threat of forced labor on the Burmese railroad turned everyone against the Japanese. But the defeat of the British in 1941 had broken the spell of white domination. In 1945, the British returned to Malaysia hoping to usher in a new colonial era. They created a crown colony out of the Federated and Unfederated Malay States together with Penang and Malacca; Sarawak and North Borneo also became crown colonies. It was soon clear, however, that their days were numbered.

3

The independence movement was triggered by a plan put forward by London in 1946 for a new form of colonial administration for the peninsula. In this proposed Malayan union, all peoples would hold essentially the same rights. The project immediately ran into opposition from the hitherto docile Malays, who were indignant at the idea of parity. Already feeling like Strangers in Their Own Land, as one slogan put it, the Malays formed a political party, the United Malays' National Organization, to make a case for special treatment. The sultans wavered and then lobbied against the plan. Faced with united Malay opposition, the British went back to their committees, and a more acceptable formula emerged over the next two years. The British, however, were still thinking in terms of a self-governing colony, while the newly politicized Malays—and increasingly, the Chinese and Indians— began pressing for self-rule to be taken to its logical conclusion: independence.

Independence for Malaya might well have come sooner than it did had not the wartime anti-Japanese guerrilla fighters of the Malayan Communist party (MCP) attempted to take over the government by force. Officially designated as an emergency, the bitter guerrilla conflict that began in 1948 lasted 12 years. A key technique of the guerrillas, the vast majority of whom were ethnic Chinese, was to attack isolated plantations and police stations from jungle sanctuaries. British High Commissioner Sir Henry Gurney was among the 2,500 civilian victims killed by the Malay Communist party, and for many years no planter went out of his home without a weapon.

By degrees, the British eliminated guerrilla activity from peninsular Malaysia except in the far north, partly by mounting military attacks, partly by removing rural Chinese—who would otherwise have supplied the fighters— to new villages well clear of the action. As the guerrilla fighters lost ground, the morale of the MCP weakened. The party had never been supported by the Malay peasantry or most of the Indian workers, and it eventually lost Chinese backing too. By the mid-1950s, most of the rebels had either surrendered or had been captured, although it was not until 1960, three years into independence, that the state of emergency was finally declared at an end. The MCP has never surrendered, however. In the late 1980s, its much-depleted forces were operating from underground bases in the difficult terrain just north of the Malaysian-Thai border, and a few hundred were still roaming around in West Malaysia.

By the mid-1950s, when the British had contained the guerrilla threat, they recognized that they would have to heed the demands for independence. Empires were crumbling fast. The French had already left that part of the world; the Portuguese still held East Timor, and the Dutch, Irian Jaya, but the only colonies of any significance in the region were held by the British. Having stamped out communism, the colonial authorities felt confident that they would be handing the country over to reliable heirs. Negotiations on a constitution for an independent Malaya began in earnest.

The British would not budge on equal citizenship rights for all ethnic groups; by now it had become clear to everyone that the Chinese and the Indians were in Malaya to stay. Mao Tsetung had declared the People's Republic of China in 1949, and the majority of Malaya's Chinese were not prepared to live under a Communist regime or to forgo the economic advantages they had acquired for themselves. For the first time, they saw Malaya as home and looked forward to full membership in an independent nation.

The British were, however, forced by the Malay's political strength to provide special privileges for the Malays in the Constitution. Enormous tracts of agricultural land were reserved for Malays, and they were granted preferential access to jobs in the civil service. Malay was recognized as the national language, and Islam was designated the state religion, to be used on formal state occasions. This did not mean, though, that Malaysia would become an Islamic state, in which Islamic law would apply to all inhabitants. Although the Constitution defined a Malay as, among other things, a person who embraces Islam, the other ethnic groups were guaranteed freedom of worship. The nine sultanates were retained, and a unique rotating kingship was established. Each of the nine royal houses was to hold the kingship for five years in turn.

The delicate negotiations over the Malay privileges were completed in June of 1957, and two months later, the independence of Malaya was announced. It became a federal democracy composed of 11 states—the nine sultanates plus the former Straits Settlements of Malacca and Penang.

Hardly had Malaya achieved independence when Singapore, then still a British crown colony, proposed a merger with its neighbor. In the early 1960s, the scope of the plan was extended to include the other British crown colonies, Sarawak and North Borneo, together with the sultanate of Brunei, which was a British protectorate. Even-

A CHRONOLOGY OF KEY EVENTS

c. 3000 B.C. The first of two waves of Malay peoples from southern China reaches the Malay Peninsula and the islands beyond. The second wave arrives around 300 B.C.

c. 100-1450 A.D. The peninsula is divided among many small trading states, whose religion is a mixture of Hinduism and Buddhism brought from India.

c. 1403-1511 Malacca becomes the foremost city-state in the peninsula. After a Muslim ruler ascends the throne, taking the title of sultan, Islam spreads through the region.

1511 Under Affonso d'Albuquerque, a famous navigator from Portugal *(below)*, the Portuguese conquer the city-state of Malacca.

1641 The Dutch take Malacca from Portugal. Sultanates elsewhere on the peninsula gain strength.

1786 The British East India Company acquires the island of Penang from the sultan of Kedah.

1824 The Dutch cede Malacca to the British.

1826 Britain starts to administer Penang, Malacca, and Singapore as a single unit—the Straits Settlements.

1840 English adventurer James Brooke *(above)* quells a rebellion in Sarawak against its overlord, the sultan of Brunei. As a reward, he is made raja of Sarawak in 1841; his descendants rule until 1946.

1848-1890 Tens of thousands of Chinese migrate to the Malay Peninsula to work as tin miners.

1874 Following unrest among the Chinese, two sultanates agree to accept British Residents. Over the next few decades, British advisers are installed in other sultanates *(below)*.

1881 The British North Borneo Company is granted a royal charter to administer a large territory previously under the sultan of Brunei.

1896 A federal government for Malaya is established in Kuala Lumpur.

c. 1900 Malayan plantations begin to grow rubber on a large scale. Indian laborers are brought in to tap the trees. By 1920, Malaya produces more than half the world's rubber.

1941-1942 The Japanese invade Malaya, Sarawak, and North Borneo.

1945 British rule returns to Malaya.

1946 The United Malays' National Organization (UMNO) is founded to campaign for Malay rights.

1946 Sarawak and North Borneo become British crown colonies.

1948 Chinese Communists in Malaya organize guerrilla resistance against the British, who declare a state of emergency; it does not end until 1960.

1957 Malaya achieves independence; Tunku Abdul Rahman is prime minister.

1963 The Federation of Malaysia is created. It includes Malaya, Sarawak, Singapore, and North Borneo, now renamed Sabah *(coat of arms, below)*.

SABAH MAJU JAYA

1965 Singapore leaves the federation.

1969 Race riots lead to the suspension of parliamentary rule for nearly two years.

1980 Petroleum, mainly from Sarawak, replaces rubber as Malaysia's chief export.

1986 Parliamentary elections confirm the UMNO—in power since 1969.

1987 Effective end of the Malay Communist party.

3

tually Brunei, unwilling to share its ample oil revenues, declined to join the union. North Borneo and Sarawak, initially fearful of a new form of colonialism, were won over with a number of concessions: Indigenous people would enjoy the same privileges as peninsular Malays, and funds would be set aside for the economic development of the states.

In 1963, the Federation of Malaysia, consisting of Malaya, Singapore, Sarawak, and North Borneo—now renamed Sabah—was proclaimed. In 1965, Singapore, unhappy about the entrenched position of the Malays, went its separate way, and Malaysia assumed the shape it has today.

Malaysia is an unusual Third World country in that it has remained faithful to the form of democracy bequeathed to it by its departing colonial ruler. Each of the 13 states—the original 11 plus Sarawak and Sabah—has its own elected assembly. The leader of the party or coalition that dominates in the elections becomes chief minister and nominates the state's executive council. In the nine states that have sultans, the sultan is the titular head of the state, but the executive council answers to the state assembly rather than to the sultan. The power of the states is not great: They control real-estate laws, laws affecting Muslim and Malay religious and cultural customs, agriculture, as well as some aspects of social welfare and local government. Sarawak and Sabah, as part of the incentive to join the Malaysian union, were granted a little more autonomy than the others. Notably, they wield authority over immigration, including that of Malaysian citizens from other states, thus ensuring that the *bumiputras* will retain their numerical superiority.

A multistory office building looks out of place in Kuala Lumpur's tranquil suburb of Jalan Bukit Bintang. Such oases of gracious living, once a hallmark of the capital, are giving way to high-density projects erected to house the fast-growing urban population.

In the market of Kota Bharu, a town just south of the Thai border, a vendor extracts a live chicken from a braided bamboo basket. Some farmers raise birds for sale, but these birds, like most of Malaysia's poultry, were bred on a large, specialized farm.

At the federal level, where the real power lies, there are many echoes of the British system. The king is head of state but without day-to-day executive power; he may act to dissolve Parliament, but his role is otherwise largely ceremonial. Parliament consists of two houses. Some members of the Senate—the upper chamber—are elected by the state assemblies, but the majority are chosen by the prime minister from among the nation's most eminent people. Members of the lower chamber, the House of Representatives, are directly elected. The Senate has more real power than Britain's House of Lords, but financial legislation is the province of the House of Representatives alone. The entire cabinet must be members of Parliament, and the prime minister—the government's chief executive officer—is, as in Britain, the leader of the dominant party.

The federal government has tremendous power; it wields authority over defense, law and order, finance, education, health, communications, and labor affairs. The states are largely dependent on the federal government for the allocation of funds, and their power is therefore limited. When the same party is in power at both the state and the federal levels, relations are harmonious; otherwise conflicts can arise, and they are almost invariably resolved in favor of the federal government. These occasional tensions have not been severe enough to damage the structure: Elections are fair, coups d'etat are unheard-of, and the military stays out of politics.

One of the first priorities of the leaders of independent Malaysia was to develop the economy. It would have been easy to rely on plantation products and the country's abundant natural resources—huge tin deposits, major reserves of both oil and natural gas, commercial quantities of coal, iron ore, bauxite, gold, and manganese, as well as great tracts of forest that yielded tropical hardwoods. But Malaysians were well aware that the colonial economy based on tin and rubber had tied their country to London commerce and had denied it the resilience that a range of industries or even a local processing capacity would have provided. Therefore, soon after the Malaysians gained their independence, the politicians decided to lessen dependence on the country's commodities by diversifying into manufacturing.

A lot of government money and an increasingly large portion of the country's growing national debt were staked on the success of heavy industry projects, among them pig-iron production, shipyards, cement plants, and engineering complexes. Malaysia began to export electronic components and textiles. Recently, it has even become an automobile manufacturer, in a joint venture with Japan's Mitsubishi Motor Corporation. In the late 1980s, manufactured goods brought in about one quarter of Malaysia's export earnings.

In its drive to industrialize, Malaysia feels somewhat handicapped by its small population. Almost alone among developing nations, it has resolved to encourage procreation, chiefly to create a bigger domestic market and a larger work force. Government ministers' exhortations to women to stay at home and raise children make the Chinese and Indians uneasy, since the Malays remain a largely rural people and tend to rear large families. Any boost in the population in the near future is likely to increase the proportion of Malays to more than 50 percent.

Nonetheless, Malaysia's population problems are minor compared with its neighbors'. Although the need for more workers is a matter for concern, this problem is far more manageable than an excessively large number of mouths to feed—the trouble in most of Southeast Asia. Besides, Malaysian workers make up in educational attainments what they lack in numbers. In particular, the Chinese are renown for their fierce drive to educate their families. The government has played its part in broadening skills, regularly budgeting at least 15 percent of its annual expenditure on education. Malaysians support six universities, and several of these have branch campuses around the country.

The move to industrialization notwithstanding, 30 percent of Malaysians still live on the land. In the past few decades, many Malay farmers have turned from subsistence rice growing to rubber cultivation. In the rubber and oil-palm plantations of West Malaysia, the majority of workers are still Indians. Trade-union agitation has greatly improved their lot, but conditions of near-slavery still occasionally come to light. Across the South China Sea in underpopulated Sabah, where many plantations have been established since the 1970s, the workers are mainly migrant laborers from the Philippines and Indonesia.

Jobs in mining are dwindling as world demand for tin shrinks. But tin's key place in the economy has been taken by oil and gas, which became major sources of revenue in the 1970s. Today, output is about half that of energy-rich Indonesia. There are some deposits off the eastern shore of West Malaysia and others in the seas north of Sabah, but the largest reserves are off Sarawak. Sarawak and Sabah see only 5 percent of their substantial oil revenues; the rest passes straight into the federal government's coffers.

Thanks to its natural riches and the energy of its people, Malaysia has been one of Asia's postindependence success stories. Production mounted steadily in the 1960s, reaching increases of 4 per-

cent per annum by the end of the decade. Accelerating growth continued during the 1970s, assisted by a commodities boom and burgeoning world trade. By 1980, growth rates were nearly 9 percent a year.

But unfortunately for the continuing health of the economy, the country's bureaucracy grew almost as fast as its GNP. Malaysia's federal system—in which the work of central government departments is often replicated at state level—absorbs more than the normal complement of underemployed civil servants. The nation has consequently acquired ASEAN's highest proportion of public-sector workers.

Moreover, Malaysia remains more dependent on commodities than it would like to be. A simultaneous dip in world prices for tin, rubber, and palm oil in the mid-1980s drove growth

TAPPING THE POTENTIAL OF RUBBER

At dawn, when the latex flows freely, a plantation worker taps a rubber tree by candlelight (below). After collection, the latex is mixed with formic acid to make it coagulate; then it is washed and squeezed between rollers and hung up to dry (right).

More than half of Malaysia's cultivated land is devoted to rubber, yet a century ago, not a single rubber plant grew in the country. Natives of Brazil, the trees were introduced to the peninsula by H. N. Ridley, an English botanist who developed techniques for growing them intensively on plantations.

The development of the automobile industry in the early 20th century guaranteed the success of the enterprise by creating a huge demand for rubber. After World War II, growers, facing competition from synthetics, developed more prolific strains. Malaysia maintained its position as the world's chief supplier of the natural product, currently meeting one third of global demand.

rates down and strengthened governmental resolve to diversify the economy still further.

The new wealth has not been shared equally by all Malaysians. The Chinese remain the richest group overall, paramount in the financial and service sectors. Many of them operate on an international scale, with interests in Singapore and Hong Kong as well as at home. They enjoy their wealth discreetly, plowing much of it back into the business if it is their own, and lavishing funds on their children's education. Family ties are strong, and passing businesses onto successive generations is very important.

One of the most respected Chinese businessmen is Tun Tan Siew Sin, scion of a family established in Malacca since the early 18th century. Tan's wealthy

father took care not to spoil his only son and impressed on him the virtues of hard work and financial prudence. After a career in politics that culminated with a 15-year spell as finance minister in the 1960s and early 1970s, Tan entered the corporate world at its highest level by becoming chairman of Sime Darby, ASEAN's largest company. Under Tan, Sime Darby diversified from its traditional speciality, plantations, into car sales, computer-software marketing, and commodity trading. An astute operator who could more than hold his own in any circle of world financiers, Tan attributed part of his success to his empathy for his compatriots gained through his family's long association with Malaysia.

But many Chinese made their fortunes without the benefit of Tan's background. Teh Hong Piow, the richest banker in Malaysia, is the son of a salesman born in Swatow, a city in China's Kwangtung province. Teh himself was born in Singapore, where he began his career as a bank clerk; he did not move to Malaysia until 1960. Six years later, at the age of 36, he became the youngest person ever to hold a banking license, and by the mid-1980s, his institution, Public Bank, was the largest privately owned bank in Malaysia.

At the opposite end of the scale, many Chinese are undeniably poor; some eke out a living as tailors, others as street vendors or small farmers. But overall, the Chinese live comfortably compared with the Indians, many of whom still languish on the plantations. The Malays, starting from a level far below that of the Chinese, have made the most dramatic gains of all, consolidating and extending the advantages they secured at the time of independence. They have a long way to go before they catch up with the Chinese, but they now control many important sectors of the economy, including plantation and manufacturing companies, banks, and commercial ventures. On the whole, the successful Malays live more ostentatiously than the Chinese. They buy luxury cars and expensive clothes and indulge in frequent trips abroad. Many make the pilgrimage to Mecca more than once and have apartments in London.

One of the wealthiest *bumiputra* businessmen is Syed Kechik, who has interests in property development, banking, and television. He temporarily dropped out of school at the age of 13 to become a street hawker; at 18, he took a job as a seaman on a boat bound for California and continued his education in the United States, eventually acquiring a political-science degree. After training as a barrister in London, he returned to Malaysia and became a noted lawyer and political consultant. From this prominent vantage point, he launched himself in business.

Syed Kechik is typical among Malay entrepreneurs in that he used politics as a starting point for his business career. The normal procedure is to build a network of contacts through politics and then to apply for a government license to import or manufacture items. Tan's experience notwithstanding, the Chinese business community is much more likely to remain at arm's length from politics, although many of them have found that it is advisable to bring Malays with useful connections onto their boards.

The Malays as a community have won most of their recent advantages through the ballot box. Like most Malaysians, the Malays vote for parties organized on rigidly ethnic lines. Since

3

At a tin mine in West Malaysia, a worker breaks up the earth with a high-pressure water jet. The slurry will be pumped to a plant that separates ore from gravel. After 1,500 years of extraction, Malaysia is still the world's largest producer of tin.

they are the largest ethnic group, and the rural districts where they tend to live have disproportionate electoral representation, they are assured the largest faction in the federal Parliament and in most state assemblies. Their principal mouthpiece is the United Malays' National Organization (UMNO); the smaller communities are served by the Malaysian Chinese Association and the Malaysian Indian Congress, while a number of other parties represent subsections of ethnic groups.

Yet despite the loyalties displayed, Malaysian politics are less divisive than they might appear at first sight. Although squabbles among the groups were allowed free play in the federation's early years, a coalition of the three main parties and some of the smaller ones has held power at the federal level since 1970. Similar coalitions run most of the state governments. The arrangement has generally worked well. In what appears to some people to be typical Southeast Asian fashion, everyone feels more comfortable searching for consensus within a broad-based government than with the confrontational politics of the West.

The coalitions have, nonetheless, not been a partnership of equals. The UMNO is without a doubt the supreme arbiter of policy, strengthened not only by its large constituency but also by old rivalries leading to infighting within the Chinese and Indian parties. In fact, since independence, the prime minister and all senior cabinet members have come from the Malay party.

The acquiescence of both the Chinese and Indian communities to the UMNO's continued preponderance stems at least in part from the fears generated by serious race riots in May of 1969. The main underlying cause

was Malay resentment of Chinese wealth. The riots followed a Chinese-dominated party's victory in several cities in the 1969 general elections. Chauvinist sentiments overflowed, and crowds spilled out of Malay areas in Kuala Lumpur to burn and loot and kill; Chinese and Indian shopkeepers defended themselves and retaliated. The violence lasted for several days. Among the hundreds killed were representatives of every group, but the Chinese and Indian communities suffered the greatest casualties. The government responded by imposing martial law and suspending Parliament. A National Operations Council ran the country for almost two years.

Although parliamentary rule was resumed in 1971, it is now recognized that 1969 was a pivotal date for postindependence Malaysia, holding the same emotive power that 1965 has for Indonesians. The temporary government was dominated by *bumiputras,* and it responded to the riots by taking steps that would dramatically increase the Malays' stake in the economy. As soon as parliamentary rule was reimposed, the Malays' special privileges were strengthened by legislation that made questioning of their prerogatives a se-

TEMPAT LARANGAN
PROTECTED PLACE

A sign outside a Penang naval base issues its warning in Malaysia's main languages: Malay, English, Hindi, Tamil, Jawi (Malay in Arabic script), and Mandarin. Although Malay is the official language, many Chinese and Indians cannot read it.

ditious act. Though an understandable reaction to their former economic hardships, the changes the Malays pushed through Parliament made the Chinese and Indians second-class citizens politically.

The shift in emphasis is epitomized by the difference in outlook between the two leading Malay politicians of the past few decades. Tunku Abdul Rahman, often fondly referred to as "the father of Malaysia," became the country's first prime minister in 1957 and retained his position for 13 years. Though a member of a Malay royal family—he was the 21st son of the 25th sultan of Kedah—he eschewed a narrowly Malay outlook. While accepting that each ethnic group in the country wanted to retain its own identity, he insisted that "there is too much talk about differences and not enough about our similarities." Indeed, he carried his commitment to a multiracial society into his own family, adopting a Chinese daughter and two Malay sons.

Mahathir Mohamad, who became prime minister in 1981, is by contrast a committed Malay nationalist. He first rose to prominence in the aftermath of the 1969 riots, when he wrote Tunku Abdul Rahman a long letter criticizing his administration for failing to uplift the *bumiputra* population. He was one of the first to demand a radical change in the treatment of the Malays, and he wanted to go further than other politicians. Tunku Abdul Rahman sacked Mahathir from the UMNO, and Mahathir subsequently lost his parliamentary seat. During his spell in the political wilderness, Mahathir wrote a book called *The Malay Dilemma,* which criticized Malays for demanding privileges without being prepared to work for them. When he finally attained power,

Mahathir supported many measures to push Malays into the fast track.

Well before Mahathir's rise, his predecessors had already set the process in motion by means of the New Economic Policy—a 20-year plan designed to conquer poverty by 1990 and to narrow the gap between the *bumiputras* and the Chinese. In such questions as education, transfer of assets in companies, buying up of British plantation assets, or opening of wilderness land for settlement, it was ordained that *bumiputras* would invariably receive preferential treatment. Large portions of the education budget, for example, were designated to provide scholarships for Malays to study at special residential schools. Companies were directed to employ quotas of *bumiputras* at each level of management. The target was for *bumiputras* to hold 30 percent of the overall pie, leaving 40 percent for other Malaysians and 30 percent for foreigners. As 1990 drew closer, the target proved unrealistic, but the Malays did succeed in substantially narrowing the gap.

The display of Malay assertiveness has extended beyond economic matters to touch every aspect of national life and to put other ethnic groups on the defensive. The language issue, for example, which has been the subject of heated debate since the time of independence, was profoundly affected by the new political climate. The 1969 riots gave impetus to plans to introduce compulsory Malay-language teaching at the secondary level in all state schools, a plan progressively implemented over 13 years, reaching the university level by 1983.

Other languages show no sign, however, of disappearing. At the primary level, parents still have the option of sending their children to Chinese-, Tamil-, or English-language schools. To supplement the Malay-language secondary and university teaching, many parents employ either English- or Chinese-language tutors. Others send their children overseas: 27,000 Malaysians—the majority ethnic Chinese—were enrolled in the United States in the mid-1980s, and many thousands more attended universities and business schools in Australia, Britain, New Zealand, and Canada. And despite heavy pressure to substitute Malay, English is still the means of communication in law courts, corporate boardrooms, hospitals, and university common rooms; it is also a neutral language in which people of different ethnic groups often choose to converse.

The Muslim faith has seen a resurgence in Malaysia that has synchronized with the expanding role of the Malay language. The Malays have always taken Islam more seriously than most Indonesians, whom they view as

3

being rather laggard in their Muslim duties and errant in devotion. Indonesians, in turn, find Malaysians embarrassingly pious and the religious atmosphere pervading their country stifling. The gap has widened in recent years. To an extent that baffles the Indonesians, Malay culture increasingly seeks inspiration from the worldwide Islamic community. Malay girls, for example, now often cover their hair with light headdresses. Until forbidden by the government in 1985, some female civil servants and university students even adopted the full, black purdah native to the Middle East, which covers all but the eyes. International Koran-reading contests draw the crowds to Kuala Lumpur's gleaming new Islamic Center, whose austere, pointed archs reflect Middle Eastern inspiration and contrast sharply with the more eclectic architecture of religious buildings from earlier eras.

In recent years, Islam has become more and more politicized. The Partai Islam SaMalaysia, the country's Islamic party, rapidly gained electoral support among Malays in the 1970s. To meet the challenge head on, the moderate UMNO decided in 1984 to describe itself as an Islamic party. For justification it could point to the constitutional clause that equates being Malay with being a Muslim. To gain some Islamic credentials, the UMNO-dominated government spent millions to establish an International Islamic University near Kuala Lumpur. It has also sent hundreds of civil servants on seminars to discuss ways of instilling Islamic values into the administration. Although such steps have been taken partly to head off more extreme Islamic movements, non-Muslims are deeply suspicious of them.

Religion underpins the traditional function of the nine sultans who, despite some predictions to the contrary, show no signs of being left behind by Malaysia's rapid industrial and social changes. Malays remain grateful for the sultans' role in securing Malay privileges in the constitution and value the link with the past that they represent. The myths and much of the prestige surrounding the sultans have gradually withered over the years, but pomp and extravagance still survive. Their regalia—sacred kris swords, ancient drums, and clarionets—are accorded reverence; on state occasions the sultans continue to dress in royal yellow and are surmounted by yellow umbrellas, a pre-Islamic symbol of authority.

Their official prerogatives include regulating the religious duties of Malays. In some states, their interpretation of Islamic law has led to the arrest of adulterers, unmarried couples, and widows living with non-Muslims. Sultans also have the discretion to award titles and honors, which Malaysians regard highly. And many insist on being consulted when sizable land concessions are being negotiated. Since land sales and rentals are now the major independent source of funds for state governments, which must otherwise rely on the federal government for finance, the involvement of the sultans in land deals gives them a modicum of real power.

The sultans do not entirely conform to the dutiful constitutional role played by the monarchs of such nations as Japan and Britain, and their numbers make them a force to be reckoned with. "There are about 25 monarchs left in the world," a recent Malaysian prime minister commented ruefully, "and half of them are in Malaysia." A few of them enjoy treating chief ministers as mere courtiers and consider themselves above the law.

In the late 1970s, a number of sultans seriously abused their relations with the state governments. Although the Constitution stated that they must assent to bills passed by state assemblies, it gave no time limit; the sultans of Johore and Perak, both due to become king in the course of the 1980s, used delaying tactics to ease state ministers out of office. Concerned that even graver iniquities might occur at the federal level when one of these headstrong leaders became king, the federal government passed a bill in 1983 that obliged the rulers at both federal and state levels to give their assent to legislation within 15 days. The move brought Malaysia close to a constitutional crisis. The king refused to sign the constitutional amendment, which all the sultans saw as a grave slur on their dignity.

Eventually, a compromise was worked out. The king was granted the right to send a bill back to Parliament once for reconsideration, after which he was obliged to sign it promptly. The sultans made a verbal agreement not to intervene in state politics: Their honor was saved, but they had learned their lesson. In 1984, the sultan of Johore ascended the Malaysian throne. Despite the federal government's earlier fears, he restricted his public role to that laid down by the Constitution.

Although the continued existence of the sultans serves as a reminder of the strength of Malay culture in multiethnic Malaysia, their popularity is not confined to Malays. Recently, the sultans won unexpected support from non-Malays unhappy about the prospect of too much power concentrated in the hands of politicians.

The masters of the new Malaysia have never apologized for their ready use of security legislation. The government's powers include wide discretion to declare localized states of emergency, to detain persons without trial or to try them in camera, to license publications, and to forbid gatherings of more than seven people. The evils the government cites in justification of such measures are the threat posed by Communist insurgency, the dangers of religious extremism, and drug abuse. Communism is well in hand now, but religion remains an explosive issue, and the drug problem is serious. Malaysia is on the smuggling route by which heroin grown in Burma reaches the West. The country's increasingly wealthy youths—many of whom are disoriented by the rapid social change brought about by economic growth—have turned in large numbers to narcotics, and Malaysia now has 400,000 addicts. To contain the problem, the death penalty is imposed for trafficking, and possession of certain amounts of drugs, including marijuana, constitutes legal proof of guilt.

Despite what many people see as an excessively harsh response to social maladies, constitutionally guaranteed liberties make Malaysia a freer place than most of its neighbors. The country's complicated federalism accommodates its diversity, allowing an impressive pluralism of thought, religious persuasion, and political affinity.

Malaysia's heterogeneous society is seen at its best on traditional holidays—the Chinese New Year, the Hindu festival of Deepavali, and Hari Raya, the Islamic celebration of the end of the fasting month. On Hari Raya, the country's Muslims, from the prime minister to paddy laborer, receive neighbors and guests of every heritage. Spicy Malay stews and salads are placed on long tables, and from morning to dusk, often for several days in a row, lines of visitors help themselves. It is an occasion for patching up old quarrels and for asking forgiveness, for reflections on the year past, and resolutions for the future. The conversation is light but touches on matters most central to Malaysians, Muslim or non-Muslim.

At Chinese New Year and Deepavali, members of the other cultures take their turns at being hosts. Once again, the disparate strands of a complex nation draw together in a spirit of tolerance and amity. □

THE SINGAPORE SUCCESS STORY

Named after the founder of Singapore, the century-old Raffles Hotel preserves the graciousness of colonial days in its classical facades and immaculate greenery. Behind it rises Raffles City, an ultramodern skyscraper complex that includes one of the world's tallest hotels.

In January 1819, Sir Stamford Raffles, a high official of Britain's East India Company, sailed the South China Sea in search of a suitable site for a trading settlement that could be developed into "a great commercial emporium and a fulcrum whence we may extend our influence politically." His quest ended on a diamond-shaped, predominantly flat island at the tip of the Malay Peninsula, about half a mile from the mainland and just one degree north of the equator. It was called Singapura, or "Lion City"—a name acquired, according to legend, when a 12th-century Sumatran prince encountered on its shores a black-faced tiger, which he mistakenly identified as a lion.

Ostensibly, Singapore was an improbable choice for Raffles to make. The island was almost entirely covered by dense jungle and mosquito-infested mangrove swamps. It was inhabited by a few hundred Malay fishermen and traders, and a considerably greater number of tigers and crocodiles. According to Raffles, the banks of Singapore's principal river were strewn with hundreds of skulls belonging to the victims of pirates. In its favor, however, were excellent deepwater anchorage and natural harbors on its southern shore; moreover, the island was located halfway along the principal trade route between India and China. Commanding an entrance to the Indian Ocean, the South China Sea, and the Java Sea, its location would enable it to become the main entrepôt of Southeast Asia.

Today, Raffles' phrase "a great commercial emporium" accurately describes the independent city-state of Singapore. The island, a mere 239 square miles in area, is approximately twice as large as the triangular-shaped Martha's Vineyard, and less than one fifth the size of Rhode Island. It has no natural resources besides its harbor and the considerable enterprise of its 2.6 million inhabitants. Yet the island is a major financial, industrial, and communications center, as well as a key post for the transshipment of commodities, especially oil from Indonesia, and rubber and tin from Malaysia. Singapore has become the world's second busiest port, after Rotterdam; it is also Southeast Asia's largest petroleum-refining center, containerport, and shipbuilding and repair center. Every year, the port handles more than $100 billion worth of trade and is used by more than 300 international shipping lines. Each month, its modern airport handles about 700,000 passengers and some 22,000 long tons of air cargo.

In the course of a year, the number of tourists visiting Singapore exceeds the number of inhabitants—primarily because it is a duty-free paradise for shoppers and gourmets. Whether they are looking for antique Chinese porcelain or the latest electronic equipment, crocodile-skin handbags or designer shirts, snake steak, or French cuisine, Singapore fulfills their desires.

4

Thanks to its commercial success, Singapore has the highest standard of living in Asia—after Brunei and Japan. Virtually the whole population shares in the prosperity: Singapore has few slums, almost no beggars, minimal unemployment, and a life expectancy of 75 for women and 70 for men. By most criteria, it is a developed nation.

Physically, this dynamic state bears little resemblance to the island where Raffles landed. Throughout Singapore, tropical forest has given way to concrete jungle, relieved by manicured oases of greenery and crisscrossed by more than 1,875 miles of highways that are bordered by grass and flowering shrubs. The towering office buildings and sumptuous hotels, as well as the overpasses, cable cars, and drive-in theaters, are thoroughly Western in style. In the harbor, the sampans and junks of local traders are far outnumbered by giant supertankers and containerships.

There are still a few Malay *kampongs*, villages of stilt houses thatched with palm leaves and surrounded by fruit trees. But more than 70 percent of Singapore's population now lives in 10- and 20-story apartment complexes that are subsidized by the government. The developments are built in clusters, forming self-contained minitowns with their own shopping districts, movie theaters, playgrounds, and community centers. For many years, construction has been maintained at a rate of one new living unit every 17 minutes. Singapore's phenomenal expansion even creates new living space out of the ocean: Since the 1960s, the land area has grown by some 13 square miles as a result of ambitious reclamation projects that dredge soil from the sea.

Malays have long since ceased to be the dominant ethnic group. The pop-

Laundry and vigorous weeds sprout from the upper floors of decrepit Chinese tenements. A few streets of such buildings have been preserved as tourist attractions, but most of Singapore's old dwellings have been razed and replaced by skyscrapers.

ulation of Singapore is 76 percent ethnic Chinese, 15 percent Malay, and 7 percent Indian; Eurasians and other groups make up the rest. Near the main port area in the southwest is Chinatown, with narrow winding lanes congested with pushcart traders and flanked by two-story shops; around Serangoon Road in the north of the city, Indians in saris and dhotis predominate. But the Chinese and Indians, like the Malays, have largely been relocated to apartment complexes, causing the old ethnic communities to break down.

A confusing babel of languages prevails. Hakka, Hokkien, and Cantonese dialects of Chinese are heard on the streets, and there are four official tongues as well—Mandarin, English, Malay, and Tamil—in which all official documents are published. English is increasingly the lingua franca; it is the main language of business, government, and education. Since Malay is the language of the indigenous people, however, it receives special mention in the constitution: The government is urged to safeguard and foster it.

Culturally, too, Singapore is eclectic. There are Hindu temples, Muslim mosques, Buddhist sanctuaries, Christian cathedrals, Jewish synagogues. Sports fans can enjoy such Western pursuits as golf, horse racing, polo, and cricket; the city-state offers an equal wealth of Eastern diversions, including Chinese street opera, snake charmers, and an annual Dragon Boat Festival.

Near the mouth of the river where Raffles originally landed stands a bronze statue of the man "to whose foresight and genius Singapore owes its existence and prosperity." It is an unstinting tribute, but hardly more than the city's remarkable founder deserves. Raffles, a

A Chinese woman places a call at a public telephone. There are about 40 telephones for every 100 Singaporeans—the highest count in Asia outside Japan—and local calls from private installations are free.

self-educated man, joined the East India Company as a clerk and rose rapidly in the hierarchy. In 1811, at the age of 30, he became lieutenant governor of the Dutch East Indies when they were occupied by the British during the Napoleonic Wars. He instituted many reforms to improve the conditions of the native population—so many that his superiors, alarmed at the expenses he was incurring, recalled him. Undaunted, Raffles sought an alternative base for British interests and eventually focused his efforts on the island of Singapore.

Within one week of sighting this future metropolis, Raffles negotiated for the British the right of settlement in return for regular annual payments to the island's territorial chief and to his overlord, the sultan of Johore. Under the terms of a new treaty, the main island, together with 54 adjacent islets, was ceded outright to Britain in 1824.

Before the advent of Singapore, the Dutch had monopolized trade in the region. Raffles made Singapore a free port, and his move rapidly destroyed

the Dutch hold. In 1825, Singapore's trade was worth £2.5 million (several billion dollars in today's terms). Forty years later, it had expanded sixfold. And at the end of the century, Malaya's great tin and rubber booms brought new wealth to Singapore.

The prosperous island needed far more labor than could be supplied by the indigenous Malay population. Malays migrated to the island from the mainland and from Indonesia, Indians came as traders and laborers, and large numbers of Chinese indentured laborers were also brought in. The first census of 1824 showed a population of nearly 11,000, with the Malays in the majority, but by 1860, more than 60 percent of the population was Chinese. By 1911, when Singapore's population exceeded 250,000, the Chinese made up nearly 75 percent of the population—a proportion maintained to the present day.

In the heyday of the British Empire, the cosmopolitan port of Singapore represented a haven of civilization to the expatriate rubber planters of Malaya. Their favorite haunt was the Raffles Hotel, which survives to this day. Although now considerably modernized and enlarged, it preserves a certain venerable charm with its stuccoed, neoclassical pillars and huge potted plants; it is also known for its celebrated invention, the cocktail called the Singapore Sling, which is one half gin, one quarter cherry brandy, one quarter tropical fruit juices, and a dash of Cointreau and Benedictine. During the 1920s and 1930s, the hotel numbered among its distinguished regulars the writer W. Somerset Maugham, who gathered material for many of his stories from loquacious guests.

Other than the Raffles Hotel, there

4

are few remaining relics of Singapore's luxurious European area, which had presented a sharp contrast to the cramped, vigorous world of Chinatown and the leisurely paced Indian quarter. The rest of Singapore was in the days of the British Empire a city of beggars and prostitutes, sweatshop cottage industries, and cutthroat wheeler-dealing. Crime was organized and controlled by Mafia-style Chinese secret societies that engaged in open gang warfare. As late as 1932, children could be sold as household slaves and concubines.

The start of World War II in Europe did not have an immediate impact on life in the city-state. Protected by a formidable naval base and a large army garrison, it seemed an impregnable fortress. But early in the morning of December 8, 1941—just one day after the bombing of Pearl Harbor had brought the United States into the war—Japanese navy planes launched an air raid for which the city, still blazing with lights, was totally unprepared. Within days, word reached Singapore that the Japanese were thrusting south through Malaya. Despite this intelligence, General Percival, the commanding officer, refused to have Singapore's northern beaches fortified. Batteries of guns still pointed out to sea in the south, in anticipation of a naval attack.

Early in January 1942, air raids were hitting Singapore almost daily, but night after night in the ballroom of the Raffles Hotel, colonials continued to dance behind blackout blinds, singing "there'll always be an England." When General Archibald Wavell, the new Far East commander, arrived, he imposed a belated sense of urgency. He ordered that northern fortifications be built and that the bulk of the British land forces be assembled on the northeast beaches

to confront the threat from the mainland. The Japanese launched their invasion on February 8—but on the northwest shore.

The Japanese found Singapore hopelessly ill-prepared. One million people were cornered in a city that was running short of food, water, ammunition, and gasoline. And so, on February 15, when plans for evacuation by sea were still confused, General Percival was authorized to surrender. Sir Winston Churchill called it "the worst disaster and largest capitulation in British history." Troops and British civilians alike were consigned to three and a half years in the island's infamous Changi prison camp or as laborers in the jungles of Southeast Asia.

Even though the Allies returned in 1945 to liberate Singapore, the great debacle wiped out the mystique of white colonial rule forever. The cry for independence grew. Britain was slow to heed the call for self-determination, continuing to perceive Singapore as a key strategic outpost and a vital communications center. Moreover, it was not clear to the British what form independence would take. The colony was so economically dependent on Malaya that the British did not believe it was capable of developing into a viable, independent state. Nor did they consider that an island with such a formidable Chinese majority could ever exist harmoniously within the framework of a Malay-dominated federation.

A measure of self-government was granted in 1954. As a result, political activity increased markedly and a number of new parties emerged; the most notable among them was the vigorous, left-wing People's Action party (PAP). The demand for further reform grew until, in 1959, Singapore was granted

At the Chinese New Year, celebrants manipulate a cloth dragon in pursuit of a pearl. The dragon represents the world's terror, the pearl its beauty; much as the dragon may squirm, it is never quite successful in swallowing the gem.

4

full internal self-government, with Britain retaining control of the island's foreign affairs and defense.

The first elections held under this new constitution resulted in a massive mandate for PAP, whose platform included total independence for Singapore and a merger with Malaya. The party wanted to become part of a larger unit, not only for the sake of political stability but for the economic benefits that a large market would provide for the island's developing industries. Singapore joined the Federation of Malaysia at its inception in 1963.

The marriage was not a success. The common market, which would have benefited Singapore's manufacturers, failed to materialize within the federation. And, as many had predicted, Singapore could not reconcile itself to the privileges accorded to Malays in the Malaysian constitution. The country had hoped that Malaysia would relax its position on this issue, but the opposite happened: Malays in Malaysia grew alarmed at the increased proportion of Chinese in the enlarged federation. After only two years—a period that was marked by a variety of disagreements—Singapore agreed to withdraw from the union. On August 9, 1965, it became a sovereign nation.

Having begun its history under the command of one outstanding individual, Singapore found another remarkable leader to take it through its first decades of independence. In 1923, Lee Kuan Yew was born into a wealthy Chinese family in Singapore. Educated at Raffles College (which has since been incorporated into Singapore University) and at Cambridge, he made his mark on the island after World War II as a labor lawyer. In 1954, he became

involved in organizing PAP. Five years later, when Singapore was accorded internal self-government, Lee became the nation's first prime minister. He was to remain at the helm for more than a quarter of a century.

Noting PAP's tenacious hold on power, commentators have frequently described Singapore as a "benevolent dictatorship." Among independent Singapore's first acts were measures to curb potential opposition. The government adapted existing British colonial legislation under which any suspected Communists and political opponents of the government could be detained indefinitely without trial or banished for lengthy periods to nearby islands. Illegal strikes were made a criminal offense, and strikes were unlawful if they were not backed, through secret ballot, by a majority of union members, or if the relevant dispute was before the Industrial Arbitration Court.

In the 1968 national elections, PAP won control of all seats in Parliament, a monopoly it maintained until 1981, when Ben Jeyaretnam of the middle-of-the-road Workers' party found himself providing the sole opposition in a 79-member parliament. In the general election three years later, PAP's share of the vote fell from 75 percent to 64 percent, and a second opposition member took his seat in Parliament. Otherwise, the power of Lee's administration remained unchallenged for more than two decades.

Officially, Singapore is designated a parliamentary democracy. More than a dozen opposition parties are registered. In addition, elections are held at least every five years, and voting is compulsory for citizens over 21. However, Singapore's democracy has serious limitations. Television and radio are gov-

1819 Sir Stamford Raffles *(below)*, an agent of the British East India Company, founds a trading post on the island of Singapore. Chinese and Malays are encouraged to settle.

1824 A treaty with local rulers gives full sovereignty to the company. Raffles' encouragement of free trade brings a rapid increase in shipping.

1826 Singapore, Malacca, and Penang are formed into the Straits Settlements.

1836 For the first time, Chinese outnumber Malays in Singapore.

1867 Singapore becomes a British colony.

1869 The opening of the Suez Canal boosts trade.

1911 The proportion of Chinese reaches 72 percent and stabilizes.

1942-1945 Japan occupies Singapore.

1959 The People's Action party, led by Lee Kuan Yew, forms the majority in Singapore's first fully elected assembly.

1963 Singapore joins Malaya, Sarawak, and Sabah to create Malaysia.

1965 Fearing Malay domination, Singapore withdraws from the federation to become an independent republic.

1970-1982 Singapore averages an annual economic growth rate of 8.5 percent.

1985-1987 In a crackdown on dissidents, the press, the Catholic Church, and the academic community, Singapore reaffirms its non-Communist stance.

A 19th-century lithograph, depicting a presentation to a visiting dignitary in 1846, captures the nucleus of Singapore and the busy harbor beyond. Founded only 27 years earlier, the British settlement had acquired some 50,000 inhabitants and an important slice of the region's trade.

ernment controlled, and no one may publish a newspaper or magazine without an annually renewed government license. The government can call a general election with less than two weeks' notice, and the opposition parties, although they may present their policies, are allowed only limited radio and television time. Such constraints restrict the opportunities of opposition parties to circulate their viewpoints.

More significantly, perhaps, PAP has created the means to ensure that its own ideas permeate Singaporean society at every level. All labor-union leaders are party members, and the majority are also members of Parliament. Every electoral constituency has a Citizens' Consultative Committee, made up of community leaders who act as liaisons between the people and their parliamentary representative; each

neighborhood has its own subcommittee. The stated purpose of this network is to ensure that the people's needs are channeled upward, to government officials. But the local representatives have to be approved by PAP, and they tend to be aspirants to professional political office. Often the committees control access to government housing and public employment, and dissenters from the party line can find themselves discriminated against in the competition for homes and jobs.

Despite the advantages that PAP has granted itself, an overwhelming reaction against the party could still be expressed at the ballot box. The party's continuing strength reflects genuine support—a token of its undeniable achievements, especially in the economic sphere.

Pragmatism has characterized PAP's approach to the economy from the beginning. In 1959, when Singapore became self-governing, the Western world feared that under a socialist leadership, the city-state would be easy prey to creeping communism in Southeast Asia. But Lee recognized that the interests of the island, as a free-trade center, would not be served by a rejection of capitalist principles. Thus Singapore emerged as a highly unorthodox socialist state: One that encouraged private

enterprise and unabashedly championed meritocracy.

Lee's government launched Singapore's industrial revolution in the 1960s by luring foreign investors and multinational companies with the bait of tax concessions, cheap and reliable labor, efficient public services, and political stability. In the mid-1960s, the government also prepared Singapore for its key position in the financial world by breaking up a cartel of British and local banks that had maintained a stranglehold on the island's high finance. Two Swiss-style concessions—tax exemption for depositors and strict secrecy—subsequently helped make Singapore the "Zurich of the East."

Meanwhile, the government had financed the multimillion-dollar development of Jurong, a desolate swampland in the southwest that was drained and transformed into a 12.5-million-

acre industrial park, with more than 800 factories engaged in turning out everything from shoelaces to ships. There was a strong emphasis on labor-intensive manufacturing—electronics equipment, hardware for light industry, wood products, and textiles—and in one decade, the country's per capita income more than doubled.

Then, in the late 1970s, when Singapore's average annual growth rate of 9.4 percent was one of the highest in the world, the international oil crisis caused developed countries to introduce protectionist measures. Lee and his technocrat advisers shrewdly responded by launching Singapore's so-called second industrial revolution. The emphasis was switched from labor-intensive to capital-intensive industry and from low-skill to high-technology production, such as advanced electronic components, computer hardware,

metal engineering, and oil-rig construction. The transformation was achieved chiefly through government loans, tax incentives, and help with industrial training for companies prepared to move into the designated sectors. The measures were extremely successful. Between 1979 and 1984, the growth rate averaged more than 8 percent per year.

In 1985, Singapore's growth rate suddenly dropped below zero. Trade, transportation, communications, and financial services were still growing, but construction and manufacturing had declined; oil refining and electronics were worst hit. Part of the problem was that increases in earnings were beginning to outstrip productivity gains; Singapore was ceasing to be a cheap-labor economy. Malaysia and Indonesia started to compete directly in oil refining and other industries, and Singapore could not keep up.

Characteristically, however, the citizens of Singapore rallied to combat the economic decline. Labor unions agreed to forgo wage increases. Union officials paraded with placards saying "we sacrifice for national survival," and the National Employers' Association praised the unions for their "responsibility and pragmatism." The government offered a package of concessions to business, including reductions in the cost of utilities and improvements in Singapore's infrastructure.

At this and the other junctures of Singapore's industrial progress, the government has manipulated the economy indirectly rather than through direct intervention. Few industries are in state hands. Hardly a typical socialist country in this hands-off approach to business, Singapore nevertheless offers more government-funded benefits and

services than almost any other state in Asia. Its social provisions are much more generous than those of Hong Kong, that other offshore center of Far Eastern trade and finance.

Singaporeans, for example, enjoy a rudimentary pension system—the only one in Asia outside of Japan. Pensions come out of a central savings fund, which builds up from regular contributions made by both employers and employees. The employees may withdraw part of their savings if they are injured or want to buy a government-built apartment, but they may not withdraw funds for any other reason until they retire. In the meantime, the fund provides the government with more than one billion dollars a year for the financing of national development.

But the main thrust of PAP's socialism has taken the form of massive investments in education, health care, and housing. Singapore has the most advanced system of state-owned and state-subsidized hospitals in Southeast Asia, providing medical care for only nominal fees. The public housing system is the envy of many a developed country, with more than 7 out of 10 families owning or renting an apartment in the clusters of government-built high-rises that have sprung up like white megaliths across the island.

A first-class education is offered to all children of elementary-school age. School attendance is still voluntary, but Singaporeans' aspirations to better their families are such that primary education is universal. Two thirds of Singapore's children—a higher proportion than in any other ASEAN country—progress to high schools. Children find themselves in an intensely competitive atmosphere, exacerbated by their being tracked according to

ability at the age of nine. Many traditional habits of deference and conformity have been overshadowed by this emphasis on personal achievement.

Singaporeans are being exhorted to emulate the materialist ambitiousness of the West, and at the same time they are expected to submit to major government intervention in their lives. Singapore is a schizophrenic society: dynamic and entrepreneurial, yet retaining much of the respect for government that characterizes other Asian societies. PAP often acts in a high-handed manner in pursuit of goals that are deemed to be for the ultimate benefit of the people.

In the interests of linguistic homogeneity, for example, the Singapore Broadcasting Corporation has eliminated Chinese-dialect broadcasts from its programming. It frequently buys Cantonese soap operas from Hong Kong and Taiwan, but Mandarin is dubbed into the sound tracks before the shows are presented to the people—many of whom would understand them far better in Cantonese. The audience has, however, found a way around the restricted viewing: Many Singaporeans buy special aerials so that they can receive transmissions, in dialect, from Malaysia.

The people have no recourse against forced resettlement, however, and the price they have paid for their improved living standards is the dismantling of their social milieu. But the destruction of traditional neighborhoods, besides eliminating slums, has served another of the government's aims: the lowering of barriers between the different ethnic groups. Ultimately, it is hoped, these diverse groups will all but forget their origins and see themselves simply

In front of a New York-style skyline, cargo awaits loading at the East Lagoon section of Singapore's vast containerport. The island's natural deepwater harbor can provide anchorage for over 400 ships at a time.

95

4

as Singaporeans. The government has grounds for optimism. There is still little intermarriage, but racial tension, which in 1964 erupted in riots, is at an all-time low.

To the outsider, particularly a person who knew Singapore in its prewar days, one of the most notable aspects of the new housing developments is cleanliness and tidiness. In general, Singapore is the most ordered city in Asia, largely as a result of strictly enforced legislation. In every neighborhood the trash is collected seven days a week. Main streets and parks are spotless, thanks to heavy fines for littering or allowing dogs to foul public places, and even the harbor is free of floating garbage and oil slicks.

With similar efficiency, the pests that transmit diseases have been almost completely eliminated; it is now an offense to leave neglected areas of stagnant water that are likely to encourage

At a Sunday morning songbird concert, an owner rewards one of the chorus with a tidbit. Breeding birds for their voices is a popular and sometimes profitable hobby among Singapore's Chinese; a fine set of vocal chords can raise the value of a pet by several thousand dollars.

the proliferation of mosquitoes and flies. Early in the 20th century, Singapore had a yearly average of 2,000 deaths from malaria. Now only a few cases of the disease are reported each year. All other tropical diseases have also been brought under control. Singapore is one of the few countries in Asia where the tap water is safe to drink. In addition, the air is wholesome. Smoking is prohibited in many public places, and tobacco advertising is banned. There are also penalties for excessive emissions from the exhaust systems of motor vehicles.

Without a doubt, the inspiration for much of the legislation to clean up the city came from Lee Kuan Yew, an extremely fastidious man known to bathe twice a day, frequently change his shirt, check the temperature of rooms he entered, carefully watch his diet, keep fit with jogging and exercises. It is said that he abhorred tobacco to such a degree that no Singaporean was permitted to smoke in his presence.

A large and efficient police force ensures that the population follows the rules governing sanitation and litter. The police have also scored notable successes in the fight against crime, which dwindled rapidly in the decade following independence. By the early 1980s, only 1 out of 22,000 Singaporeans fell victim to a violent crime during the course of a year, compared with 1 out of 47 New Yorkers. The criminal activity of Chinese secret societies has virtually ceased, and nowhere else in Asia has corruption been brought under greater and more effective control.

The moral well-being of Singaporeans is as well protected as their property. Very strict pornography laws have been passed: Films judged to depict explicit sex or excessive violence are

A young family eats out at one of Singapore's innumerable food stands. At one time, the island was full of outdoor snack bars, but now a hygiene-conscious government confines all such cheap fast-food counters to indoor shopping malls.

banned or edited, and tourists have been fined for possession of *Playboy* magazine. Government employees have been fined or sacked for wearing their hair over their collars, and many tourists in the late 1960s and early 1970s had to submit to a trim at the airport before they were allowed to enter the country.

More controversially, the Singapore government maintains a strong—some would say intrusive—policy over family planning. The need for a birth-control policy became evident soon after independence. Between 1948 and 1958, Singapore's population had doubled, and by 1965, the annual growth rate was more than 30 per 1,000. The government reacted not only by publicizing contraceptive methods and making abortion easily available but by penalizing large families. The tax relief given for first and second children dropped markedly for a third child, and women did not receive paid maternity leave on the birth of a fourth. Workers who agreed to be sterilized received an extra week's annual vacation.

The campaign was extremely effective: By the early 1980s, the annual birth rate had fallen to 17.3 per 1,000. But by that time, the government seemed anxious to influence not only the number but the quality of the new generation. In 1983, Lee censured the well-educated youth of Singapore for avoiding or postponing marriage and children in their relentless pursuit of a career and material rewards. Since the less educated were more likely to reproduce, a skewed pattern of births was emerging. One of the measures introduced to correct the perceived imbalance was a financial inducement for a woman to be sterilized if the family income and educational attainments were low. But there was so much opposition to this policy that it has since been abandoned.

Some observers of Singapore find it so clinically clean and well ordered, so puritanical and repressive, as to be reminiscent of the society depicted in Aldous Huxley's novel *Brave New World,* where social engineering from the womb to the tomb disregards spiritual values and diminishes human individuality. The same view is expressed in certain circles in Singapore. One university lecturer has written:

One notes a tendency on the part of the government leaders, including the prime minister, to view people as digits, buttons to be pressed, gears to be shifted, cogs, units that can be plugged into systems, or beings without moral volition who have to be moved by carrots or sticks.

To the majority in Singapore, however, the new prosperity outweighs the less agreeable aspects of life. Indeed, it is a tribute to successive PAP governments that the principal grievances today address competitive education, puritanical regulations, overregimentation, and intrusion into private life, whereas once they were about food and shelter, social injustice, and crime. Moreover, social controls that seem oppressive to the Western world may well be appropriate in the unique circumstances of Singapore. In all his years as prime minister, Lee Kuan Yew never forgot the vulnerability of his tiny, almost resourceless island state. He extolled the necessity for discipline, the need to climb ever higher up the economic ladder. "You will not drop down on a soft paddy field," Lee believed. "It is hard, hard concrete. Your bones are broken, and it's *kaput.*" □

Neon-striped escalators and Chinese lanterns decorate a spacious air-conditioned shopping mall. Such complexes act as magnets for the three million tourists who visit Singapore each year—primarily from Australia, Japan, Britain, and neighboring Southeast Asian countries.

5

A doleful eye weeps expressively
down a foglamp of a Manila jeepney.
Lovingly decorated, these trucks are
the capital's principal mode of public
transportation. Successors to U.S.
Army jeeps, they were converted by
the Filipinos into minibuses at the
end of World War II.

THE VOLATILE PHILIPPINES

To the Spaniards, who ruled the Philippines from the 16th to the 19th century, the islands were not really a part of the Orient; Spain saw them, rather, as the westernmost point on the map, the farthest outpost of the great Spanish empire in the Americas. The imperial picture became an enduring truth. Although the Filipinos live not far from the Asian landmass, descend from Malay and Chinese stock, and belong to ASEAN, they are set apart from other Asians by three centuries of Spanish rule and nearly 50 years under the United States. Filipino society hovers between East and West.

Other peoples in the region were also colonized, of course, but not so early or so thoroughly. In the Philippines, European rule was imposed before any centralized native state had emerged. The Philippines never had a chance to generate a Malaccan or a Majapahit empire. They had developed no traditions of statecraft, no courtly culture; most indigenous peoples had learned no religion other than the nature worship practiced by their far-off ancestors. They were very susceptible to new influences, and they found themselves governed in turn by two powers determined not merely to exploit the territory but to shape its people.

The uniqueness of the Philippines is less apparent today than it was 50 years ago, largely because every other Asian nation has now felt the impact of Western culture. But some striking distinc-

tions still separate the Philippines from its neighbors. Among the more notable differences are an emphasis on education and the prevalence of English—both heritages of the American era. In the Philippines, one quarter of those between the ages of 20 and 24 attend a university or college. Literacy is, at 87 percent, as high as Singapore's and higher than that of most Asian countries. The archipelago has 77 native languages, of which one, Tagalog, is the basis of the official national language, Pilipino. But English is taught in schools as the universal second language, and everybody speaks at least a smattering of it.

Another peculiarity of the Philippines is its religion: It is the only predominantly Christian nation in Asia. The Spaniards converted most of the Filipinos to Roman Catholicism 400 years ago; in this century, American missionaries spread the Protestant faith among the remote tribal peoples. Today, 85 percent of the population is Catholic, 4 percent worships in the schismatic Philippine Independent Church, which observes Catholic rites, and another 4 percent is Protestant.

Almost every town of standing in the Philippine islands is dominated by a florid baroque church. Parish churches are the hub of community life, and priests and bishops command great authority. The great folk festivals, often attended by hundreds of thousands of participants, are as crowded and color

On the island of Negros, sons of Communist sympathizers tote toy rifles, reflecting through play the violence that stalks the Philippines. During the mid-1980s, more than 15,000 Communist guerrillas were active throughout the countryside.

ful as those of Indonesia or India, but the images that are carried in procession are those of Spanish saints, and they would not be out of place during Holy Week in Seville.

Enthusiasm is the hallmark of Catholicism in the Philippines. The faithful crowd the churches to pray before brightly colored portraits of saints and to light candles in profusion to their heavenly protectors. On Good Friday, some *penitentes* have themselves bound to crosses, and some even have their hands pierced with nails, to act out Christ's Passion.

The Spaniards not only gave most Filipinos their religion, but they molded the very structure of society. They created a feudal hierarchy, totally alien to the cooperative traditions of Southeast Asia, which has never been entirely discarded. As a result, abject need—a rarity even in poor countries elsewhere in the region—is widespread in the Philippines. However, those at the upper end of the economic scale possess extraordinary wealth, power, and opportunity for corruption.

Not surprisingly, Philippine politics have long been troubled and unstable. Most Filipinos take an intense interest in public affairs—to the point of insurrection if the path of democratic opposition is blocked. In this area, too, they show themselves different from the Southeast Asian norm. In neighboring countries, dissent may be glossed over in an attempt to reach a workable consensus. In the polarized society of the Philippines, however, dissent will always come to the fore.

Discord is not a modern phenomenon in these tropical islands. According to myth, it engendered the very land itself. A creation legend describes how the islands of the archipelago were churned up from the ocean floor in the course of an argument between the sea and the sky—a dispute fomented by a mythical bird that was looking for a place to roost.

Many of the 7,107 islands that make up the nation are, in fact, little more than bird rookeries: Only about 1,000 are inhabited. Eleven islands constitute 94 percent of the total land area, which equals 115,830 square miles. The most important are Luzon in the north, Mindanao in the south, and between them, the Visayan group, which includes Cebu, Palawan, Samar, Negros, Leyte, Panay, and Bohol. Although the Philippines is comparable in area to Italy or the British Isles, its aggregate coastline is nearly as long as that of the U.S.

The Philippine islands are among the most beautiful in the world—not least because most of them are clustered within sight of others, so that almost every palm-fringed coast affords a view across an azure sea to another island in the distance. The shallow waters between are a rich source of fish, and a large portion of the Philippines' protein comes from the sea. Most of the larger islands have rugged interior uplands that rise from 3,000 to more than 9,000 feet.

Some of the more remote mountain regions are still inhabited by Negritos, descendants of the first people to settle in the islands. Most Filipinos, however, are descended from later waves of migrants who introduced a mongoloid stock to the islands—the peoples known as proto-Malays, also from the Asian mainland, and a subsequent group of Malay settlers who probably came by way of Indonesia. By about 300 A.D., the last groups of Malay immigrants were well established in the coastal regions of the Philippines.

The ethnic mixture was further enriched by a steady flow of other newcomers, especially Chinese, who came for trade or plunder and then married island women. Muslim seafarers crossed the water from northern Borneo in the late 15th century and brought Islam to Palawan and Mindanao, where the religion of Muhammad flourishes to this day. Within a century, Islam was gaining converts among the

With umbrellas raised against an expected downpour, a family heads for shelter in Sabang-an, a hamlet in the mountains of Luzon. The home-made dwellings of corrugated tin and rough-hewn planks are typical of most parts of the Philippines.

102

local rulers—known as *datus*—in settlements as far north as Luzon.

Before Islam could take a firm hold in the northern islands, the Europeans arrived. In the course of his epic bid to circumnavigate the world in the early 16th century, Ferdinand Magellan arrived in the Philippines. Magellan and some of his lieutenants were murdered by Filipinos, but the surviving men, led by Juan Sebastián del Cano, achieved the expedition's goal, making their way back to Europe via the Moluccas and the Cape of Good Hope.

Magellan had hoped to prove, on behalf of Charles I of Spain, that the Spice Islands lay in the part of the world that Pope Alexander VI had assigned to Spain when the still-unmapped continents were apportioned between Spain and Portugal. For a while, Magellan's discovery remained a bone of contention between the two rival empires. The issue was not resolved in favor of Spain until after the accession of Philip II, in whose honor the islands were renamed the Islas Filipinas.

In 1564, Spanish conquistador Miguel López de Legazpi sailed from Mexico to the Philippines with 400 men. They arrived the following year and founded the first Spanish colony at what is now the city of Cebu. Later, Legazpi established a fortified settlement on Luzon at Manila, whose magnificent harbor made it the natural focal point of the islands. Legazpi extended Spanish rule by persuading many of the local chieftains to pledge their allegiance in return for retaining their regional power as *datus*.

Although the Philippines had no spices worth exporting, the five Augustinian friars who accompanied Legazpi found the islands fertile ground for saving souls. For the next three centuries, Spanish friars were to play a decisive role in the unfolding social and economic life of the islands. Not only the Augustinians but other monastic orders—notably the Dominicans, Franciscans, and Jesuits—established missions throughout the archipelago, learned to speak the native languages,

5

introduced new crops, such as corn and cocoa from America, and taught the "civilized" tribes more efficient and productive farming methods.

Until then, most Filipinos were shifting cultivators who held land in common. The Spanish established a feudal system similar to Europe's, and the hereditary chieftains or *datus* took advantage of the Western concept of private ownership to claim much of the land for themselves. A chasm grew between the local chiefs and the landless peasants, who now had only their new religion to console them. Except for the reclusive high-mountain tribes and the Muslims of the south, whom the Spanish never succeeded in subduing or converting, all Filipinos were eventually received into the Catholic Church—though they still clung to animist modes of thought. Notable among these was the concept of a bargain struck with God: The Filipinos continued to believe that if they made some sacrifice they would then be able to ask for a specific favor to be granted.

Since most of the secular Spanish colonists congregated in Manila—in more than 1,200 villages the priest was the only Spaniard—it was the friars who came to embody the Spanish presence elsewhere in the islands of the Philippines. For the most part, they exercised a kind of benevolent despotism over the Filipinos, whom by force of Latin-American habit they called *indios*. The colonial government could hardly have functioned without the friars, who maintained order among the *indios* and reported back to Manila on what was happening in the provinces. It acknowledged this dependence by putting the priests on its payroll: They became salaried government officials. In time, religious orders and individual bishops were granted large landholdings and became enormously wealthy.

The colonial government, modeled on that of Spanish America, functioned as a subcolony of the Spanish empire in Mexico rather than as a direct dependency of metropolitan Spain. In theory, the governor general, who was appointed by the king, held almost unlimited powers. Yet he could govern effectively only with the help of the friars, as well as with a military and civil bureaucracy staffed mainly by career officers from Mexico, Peru, and Central America, who came to the Philippines to make their fortune. The tradition of using public office for private gain became ingrained; indeed, the practice persists to this day at every level of government.

Economically, the Philippines was almost wholly dependent on Mexico. Cargoes originating in Manila did not go to Spain by the shortest route, around the Cape of Good Hope: By royal decree, designed to prevent Asian goods from competing directly with Spanish products, the Philippines could export only to Mexico. Moreover, Spain also tried, with considerable success, to limit trade to two government-owned ships—called the Manila Galleons—which carried East Asian manufactured goods, mainly Chinese silks, from Manila to Acapulco once or twice a year and returned laden with silver bullion and minted coin. The profits from this monopoly sustained the Spanish community in Manila and the Chinese merchants who supplied these silks, but did nothing to stimulate local industries.

As Spanish maritime power waned during the 17th and 18th centuries, so did the port's commercial importance. In the early 19th century, the Mexican War of Independence finally forced the Spanish government to regard the Philippines as a part of the East rather than the West and to take a more active interest in the colony's affairs. Free trade replaced the old monopoly system in 1834. In the wake of increased immigration from Spain, secular culture began to make its appearance in the islands: 30 newspapers were founded between 1840 and 1872.

The Christ child in Spanish religious dress is borne aloft during a festival in Malalos, 18 miles north of Manila. The infant Jesus has been revered in the Philippines since 1521, when his image moved the pagan queen of Cebu to cry out for baptism.

A CHRONOLOGY OF KEY EVENTS

c. 3000 B.C. Malay peoples start to settle in the islands and form numerous isolated communities.

c. 1400 A.D. The people of the southern islands convert to Islam.

1521 Ferdinand Magellan claims the islands for Spain but is killed in a skirmish with native inhabitants.

1565 Spaniards conquer and begin settling lowland areas of the islands, which they name after their king, Philip II. They subsequently create vast estates for themselves and convert the Filipinos (*below*) to Catholicism.

1572-1811 The Spaniards of Manila derive great wealth from galleons that sail to Mexico, carrying oriental luxuries outward bound and silver on the return.

1821 Mexico becomes independent; the loss of this rich colony leads Spain to introduce sugar, tobacco, indigo, and hemp to the Philippines as cash crops.

1896 The Spaniards execute José Rizal, a moderate Filipino campaigner for reform, who becomes a national hero.

1896-1897 An armed revolt against Spanish rule ends in truce and the promise of reforms by the Spaniards.

1898 War breaks out between Spain and the United States (*above, right*). Confident of American support, Filipino rebel leaders declare independence. U.S. troops force the Spaniards to capitulate, but instead of backing Filipino independence, the United States takes over the islands.

1907 The U.S. sets up an elected legislature—the first in Southeast Asia.

1934 A commonwealth is established, with a constitution drawn up by Filipinos, and the United States promises to grant independence after 10 years.

1941-1945 Japan occupies the Philippines.

1946 The United States grants independence and obtains a long lease on a number of Philippine military bases.

1965 Ferdinand Marcos (*below*) is elected president.

1969 Communist guerrillas begin an escalating campaign of insurgency.

1972 Marcos declares martial law in the midst of severe economic and political troubles. It is lifted in 1981.

1983 Opposition leader Benigno Aquino is killed, bringing about Marcos's ouster.

1986 Marcos is toppled by an army revolt with strong popular support. Corazón Aquino becomes president.

1986-1987 Anti-Communist vigilante groups emerge; in April 1987, Aquino survives a fifth coup attempt.

Around this time—earlier than in Indonesia or Malaysia—the Philippines saw the emergence of an educated native-born elite. It was made up largely of *mestizos*—a Spanish word that means "of mixed blood," though it bears little of the perjorative sense of the English term "half-caste." By mid-century, about a quarter of a million Filipinos were descendants of Chinese merchant fathers and *india* mothers: They lived in their own suburb of Manila—Binondo—and dominated many different aspects of trade and agriculture. Another influential *mestizo* community—about 20,000 strong—traced its descent to Spanish or Spanish-American forebears.

Mestizo landowners played a leading role in developing sugar and indigo as export crops, and became major rice producers by leasing land from the friars and subletting it to local sharecroppers. Some of the newly affluent *mestizos* began to travel widely; a number of them went to Spain for their education. *Mestizo* intellectuals campaigned for political reforms and the abolition of the "friarocracy." The conservative Catholic establishment did its best to maintain the status quo: In 1898, the curriculum at the Church-run University of Santo Tomás in Manila was essentially the same as it had been since 1611, when the school was founded by the Dominicans. José Rizal, the Chinese-*mestizo* physician and scientist who had earned doctorates in both Spain and Germany, became a brilliant spokesman for change. He wrote two novels dealing with the abuses of Spanish rule in the archipelago—*Noli Me Tangere* in 1886 and *El Filibusterismo* in 1891—which were banned by the authorities but successfully smuggled into the Philippines to be

5

At Palo on the island of Leyte, lifelike statues set in water commemorate the fulfillment of General Douglas MacArthur's pledge to return to the land conquered by the Japanese in 1942. The ensuing year-long campaign cost the lives of thousands of Americans and one million Filipinos.

come the twin bibles of an emerging national consciousness.

Although Rizal advocated compromise and peaceful revolution, he was arrested on his return from Europe to the Philippines in 1892 and was exiled to a remote town on Mindanao. Four years later, a group of radicals launched an armed insurrection that scored some initial victories against the Spanish troops on Luzon. Rizal was brought before a military court on trumped-up charges of having conspired with the insurgents and was executed by a firing squad on December 30, 1896. The Spanish succeeded in quelling the uprising, but only by paying its leader, Emilio Aguinaldo, 800,000 pesos in cash to retire to Hong Kong with 35 of his followers.

In the meantime, the revolution that had broken out in Cuba, the other major Spanish colony, resulted in a U.S. declaration of war on Spain. In May 1898, the U.S. Asiatic squadron under Commodore George Dewey destroyed the antiquated Spanish fleet in a one-sided military engagement off the Philippines, costing Spain 380 lives and the United States only one. Aguinaldo and his men returned to the Philippines with the help of Dewey, and they liberated several towns south of Manila. In August, the small Spanish garrison of Manila surrendered to an American invasion force.

The Philippine revolutionaries were denied any part in the victory they had helped to bring about. The Americans told them they would be fired on if they entered Manila—an order that infuriated the Filipinos, who had already set up a provisional government and issued a declaration of independence. But President William McKinley had other plans. In accordance with the peace treaty that ended the Spanish-American War in December 1898, the U.S. formally annexed the islands together with Guam and Puerto Rico, and the Philippine revolution against Spain was thus transformed into the Philippine "insurrection" against the U.S. military government.

When President McKinley issued a proclamation defining American policy as one of "benevolent assimilation" in which "the mild sway of justice and right" would replace "arbitrary rule," Aguinaldo countered with a bitter denunciation of America's "violent and aggressive seizure." The army of the Philippine republic took to the highlands and held out against some of the best troops in the U.S. Army for more than two years, at a cost to the United States of about 4,200 lives. Aguinaldo himself was captured by a force of American-led Filipino Scouts in 1901, and he issued an appeal to his followers to lay down their arms.

The new civil government, initially headed by Judge William Howard Taft (afterward elected president of the United States), did its best to convince the Filipinos that the U.S. role was to be one of trusteeship and tutelage. Millions of dollars were spent on roads, harbors, medical facilities, and forestry development. Hundreds of American teachers were sent to towns throughout the islands to coach 2,500 Filipinos in English and to disseminate American ideas on education. This core group of informed Filipinos rapidly spread literacy. Taft personally conducted the delicate negotiations with Pope Leo XIII concerning the expropriation of estates owned by the Catholic friars, most of whom had returned to Spain: Eventually their lands were purchased from the Vatican for $7.2 million.

The U.S. administration, announcing that its aim was to prepare the Philippines for self-rule, also established a new judicial system and promulgated a legal code that included a bill of civil rights; in 1907, it inaugurated a bicameral Philippine legislature that had jurisdiction over regional affairs. The right to vote was initially limited to literate males—women first voted in 1938—but popular democracy took root rapidly. During World War I, the civil service was deliberately "Filipinized": By 1921, there were about 13,000 Filipino administrators and only 600 American officials.

But such gestures were not in themselves enough to ensure Philippine acceptance of the country's new masters. The United States also paid a more insidious price. Although their democratic instincts were against the feudal system that had solidified under Span-

ish rule, the Americans knew that they needed the support of the most powerful members of Filipino society—the pre-Spanish aristocracy, with their extensive landholdings, and the new educated elite, composed mainly of *mestizos*. Thus, despite Taft's original intentions to distribute the Church land in small parcels to the tenants who worked them, a considerable portion of land was eventually sold on the open market and bought by the large landowners. And, despite the spread of education, *mestizo* families were allowed a disproportionate number of the key positions in administration. In many ways, the Americans brought the Philippines into the 20th century, but they failed to overturn the islands' archaic social order.

In 1934, the United States took a decisive step toward granting independence. Congress passed legislation es-

tablishing the Commonwealth of the Philippines, an interim form of government that was to prepare the way for full independence after a 10-year period of transition. The commonwealth received a constitution and was self-governing under a Filipino president, but for the time being, foreign affairs and defense remained in American hands. The first commonwealth elections were held in 1935, and the Nationalist party candidate, Manuel Quezon, who at one time had been an officer in Aguinaldo's revolutionary army, was elected president.

Quezon's carefully laid plans for leading the nation to independence were cut short by the advent of World War II. Although he had taken the precaution of forming the Army of the Philippines and appointing retired U.S. General Douglas MacArthur as its field marshal, the Japanese attack on the U.S. fleet at Pearl Harbor on December 7, 1941, took both Filipinos and Americans by surprise. Ten hours later, the American bombers and fighter planes stationed at Clark Air Base, near Manila, were caught on the ground and obliterated by a Japanese air attack. Though deprived of air cover, MacArthur—now in command of the combined United States and Philippine forces—conducted a brave defense during the Japanese invasion of Luzon. He set up his headquarters on the island fortress of Corregidor, at the entrance to Manila Bay, and concentrated his forces on the nearby Bataan Peninsula. For more than three months, his malaria-ridden troops defended a shrinking perimeter against a numerically superior Japanese force, but their position was ultimately hopeless. Eventually, the defenders ran out of food and ammunition.

Trees and shrubs grant privacy to spacious villas in Dasmariñas village, an elite area of Manila adjoining the financial district. The gap between rich and poor is wider than in most other Southeast Asian countries; 10 percent of the Filipinos earn more than 40 percent of the income.

Makeshift ferries creep between banks of trash lining a canal in Tondo, Manila's most noisome slum. In the background are the shabby houses of its more fortunate residents; the vast majority have to live in eight-by-eight-foot cardboard shacks.

MacArthur had been ordered to Australia—promising, however, to return—by the time the general in command at Bataan surrendered on April 9, 1942. At the time of the capitulation, the defenders of Bataan numbered some 64,000 Filipinos and 12,000 Americans. At least one tenth of them subsequently died of starvation and disease, or were brutally murdered by their Japanese captors, on the grueling 60-mile forced trek to prison camp that later became known as the Bataan Death March.

A remnant of the army held out on Corregidor for another month before succumbing to heavy bombardment. The surrender of that force on May 6 officially marked the end of hostilities in the Philippines. Thousands of soldiers from units stationed elsewhere on the islands refused, however, to give themselves up; they simply melted into the jungle and mountains and formed the nuclei of guerrilla organizations. One of the most important of these was the Communist-led Hukbalahap—or Huks, for short.

Just before the fall of Corregidor, Quezon left for America and set up a government-in-exile. Most of the remaining members of the Filipino elite collaborated with the Japanese, who—anxious to enlist support in their military aims—declared the Philippines independent in 1943 and set up a puppet government under José Laurel. The country's new overlords ruthlessly stamped out any subversion, repressed religion, and requisitioned rice. From the start of the Japanese occupation, most Filipinos looked eagerly for an American deliverance. Coastwatchers risked their lives to supply the Allies with vital intelligence about Japanese shipping movements. More than a quarter of a million Filipinos eventually joined the guerrilla groups, which harassed the Japanese army of occupation so effectively that by 1944 the Japanese had control of only 12 of the archipelago's 48 provinces.

In October of that year, MacArthur fulfilled his pledge and returned to the islands, landing on Leyte with four American divisions. Eleven months of bitter fighting followed before Japan surrendered. In all, an estimated one million Filipinos lost their lives in the course of the war, a large proportion of them in the last months of combat; and the final battle for Manila left the capital one of the most extensively war-damaged cities in the world.

Although the Japanese-sponsored regime had been nominally a republic, true independence did not arrive until July 4, 1946, when Manuel Roxas was

5

sworn in as the first president. The willingness with which the U.S. agreed to transfer its remaining powers left it on cordial terms with its former colony. One consequence was that the United States was able to use the Philippines as the center for its military activities in the western Pacific. It was granted a long lease on Clark Air Base and Subic Bay Naval Base, two huge installations that it had founded in the early years of the century.

The Americans bequeathed to the Philippines a constitution modeled on their own, with a president and a bicameral legislature. During the first 20 years of independence, two parties, the Liberals and the Nationalists, alternated in power. Although the pattern superficially resembled that of United States politics, in reality it was quite different. The parties' policies were almost indistinguishable, and politicians readily shifted allegiance from one to the other if it seemed to their advantage. Those in power used their office to enrich themselves. However, elections were held regularly, and the succession of new faces at the top gave perennial grounds for hope.

The economic news also fostered optimism. At the time of independence, the Philippines was overwhelmingly agricultural, growing rice and corn as staples, and coconuts and sugarcane for export. During the 1940s and 1950s, however, the economy began to diversify. Factories making textiles, shoes, and cement appeared. Mining grew in importance. Gold had been extracted from Luzon since the 1930s, but copper production surpassed it in the early 1960s. Furthermore, the tropical rain forests in the highlands began to yield valuable quantities of mahogany and other hardwoods.

During the first eight years of independence, trade between the Philippines and the United States remained free, as in the colonial era; beginning in 1954, both countries began to raise tariffs, but it was not until 1974 that Philippine products had to compete on equal terms with other foreign goods in American markets.

The long period of preferential treatment helped the Philippines to grow at an average annual rate of 5 to 6 percent in the 1950s and 1960s—faster than many of its neighbors. But this success tempted the governments of the time to avoid facing the country's grave underlying problems—an inequitable distribution of land, a burgeoning population, and increasing violence in the cities.

The land issue surfaced soon after independence. About 60 percent of peasants owned plots, most of which were small; the other 40 percent were tenants, sharecroppers, or paid plantation workers subsisting in miserable conditions. Once again, the wartime Huk guerrillas took up arms—this time in the name of peasants' rights and land reform. After years of sporadic fighting in Luzon, Ramon Magsaysay, a former non-Huk guerrilla who became defense secretary in 1950, militarily defeated the insurgents. When he became president in 1953, he took a leaf out of the Huks' book and resettled thousands of landless peasant families from Luzon in uncrowded parts of Mindanao and Palawan. Magsaysay wanted to alter land distribution more drastically by limiting the size of holdings and selling the excess from large estates to tenants. But entrenched interests opposed him, and when he died in an airplane crash in 1957, his more ambitious plans for land reform remained unrealized.

A mountainside carved meticulously by hand into a stairway of rice terraces testifies to the labors of Ifugao tribespeople from northern Luzon. With their water-retaining dikes, the terraces have been lovingly maintained for hundreds—perhaps even thousands—of years.

5

In the meantime, population pressures were aggravating the hardships of the poor. The census of 1903 counted 7.6 million Filipinos; 60 years later, the population had risen to about 28 million, and it was growing at one of the fastest rates in the world—3 percent per annum. The explosion was largely the result of the introduction of modern public-health facilities at the turn of the century. Its effects were all the more serious because of the islands' rugged topography, which crowded people into the fertile valleys. The government, however, did not propose a public-service campaign to reduce the birthrate in the Philippines; politicians were not prepared to take on the Cath-

olic Church, which was opposed to birth control.

Violence was in part a heritage from the American era; firearms had been available with few restrictions, as in the United States, and many people had acquired guns. Landlords had taken to employing armed gangs to bully rebellious tenants. After the Americans left, street crime became a marked problem, and lawlessness escalated during the 1950s and 1960s.

In 1965, the Philippines elected a new president on the strength of his supposed ability to remedy such chronic problems as hunger, street crime, and government corruption. Ferdinand Marcos, a wartime guerrilla fight-

er and a noted trial lawyer, earned a great deal of praise during his early years in office for building irrigation systems and for introducing improvements in public health, transportation, and communications. Marcos even achieved a limited measure of land reform in central and northern Luzon. He subsequently contrived to entrench himself in power, to become the most durable and problematical—and in many quarters, the most heartily detested—politician in Philippine history.

In 1969, he became the first president to win a second term of office. The constitution then in force limited the president to two four-year terms, but outbreaks of violence and civil unrest

during the early 1970s gave Marcos a pretext for declaring martial law in 1972 and forcing through a "reform" constitution that allowed him to stay on indefinitely as head of state. Buttressed by a series of referenda on specific points of policy, he ruled by decree and kept martial law in force until 1981. When his opponents, led by Senator Benigno Aquino, accused him of wanting to establish a "garrison state," Marcos proved them right by imprisoning hundreds, and ultimately thousands, of dissidents. Aquino himself was held in detention for eight years—until May of 1980, when he was permitted to travel to the United States for open-heart surgery. In place of the Philippines' accustomed pluralism in party politics, the press, and labor unions, the country was now controlled from the center, with the army and the security services as Marcos's main instruments of power.

Meanwhile, the seeds of economic crisis were being sown. President Marcos's ambitious development projects had been financed by large loans, which in the late 1960s and early 1970s were quite cheap to maintain. But after the dramatic rise of oil prices in 1973, interest rates soared and the foreign debt of the Philippines increased to crippling levels. And to make matters even worse, a slump in world prices for all major Philippine commodities—sugar and coconuts, copper and timber—also drastically reduced the country's foreign earnings.

Many industries were by this time in the hands of Marcos's associates, who were mismanaging them with the sole intent of personal enrichment. When the industries began to fail in the early 1980s, the government bailed them out, squandering huge sums of money.

In the meantime, Marcos himself was abusing the Philippine economy on a scale only conjectured at the time. Through corrupt deals, he amassed a private fortune equivalent to one third of the national debt.

After martial law was lifted in 1981, Marcos was reelected as head of state. However, the vote for Marcos did not accurately portray the feelings of the Filipinos, because the opposition, convinced that Marcos would rig the results, had boycotted the election. But the turning point in many Filipinos' attitudes came when Benigno Aquino returned from the United States on August 21, 1983. He was shot dead at Manila Airport as he left the airplane. According to the government, the assassin was a Communist agent, Rolando Galman, who was gunned down by soldiers on the spot. The political opposition claimed, however, that the government and the military were involved in Senator Aquino's murder. A civilian fact-finding board concluded that the crime had been planned and executed by a group of conspirators that included many of the country's highest-ranking military officers. The chief of staff, General Ver, and 25 other military personnel were eventually put on trial for the shooting, but they were acquitted.

In the weeks after Aquino's murder, nervous foreign banks withdrew their funds. The Philippines found itself massively in debt to the International Monetary Fund. At first, the government refused to comply with the IMF's tough stipulations to drastically cut public spending and the supply of money. As a result of the government's mishandling of the economy, inflation topped 60 percent in 1984. When the Filipinos finally agreed to the condi-

tions, inflation began to come under control, but most sectors of the economy sank into deep recession. In striking contrast with the burgeoning growth in most other Far Eastern countries, the economy of the Philippines shrank by 5 percent in 1984 and by another 5 percent in 1985.

At the worst moments of the slump, one of the few saving graces in the economy was the generosity of Filipinos away from home. More than half a million expatriates work overseas. There are many Filipinos in the Middle East, laboring on huge construction projects, and another large population in the United States, working at jobs that range from waiter or hotel porter to doctor and university professor. In many other countries, too, Filipinos' literacy and familiarity with Western ways open doors. In 1984, the money they sent home was equivalent to 13 percent of Philippine export income.

The other bright spots in the economy were within the agricultural sector. The introduction of high-yield rice strains and hybrid corn was transforming productivity. The heavy dependence on sugar and coconuts for export earnings was being progressively lessened by new ventures in coffee, rubber, and fish farming.

But the positive bits of economic news were overshadowed by the strains of recession and the public's weariness with Marcos's long reign. Law and order began to collapse in many areas of the country. Ordinary citizens in the 1980s increasingly found themselves caught in the crossfire between armed groups of the left and right—among them, private armies recruited by corporations or industrialists, miscellaneous bands of robbers and hired killers, in addition to assorted factions

On Negros, steam and smoke belch from the chimneys of the Victorias Milling Company, one of the largest sugar refineries in the world. The island's economy has been devoted almost entirely to sugar production since the 19th century.

5

within the army and the police force.

Amid this confusion, the Communist movement grew in strength. The Communist party of the Philippines (CPP) and its military wing, the New People's Army, were established in 1969 after a breakaway from the Soviet-backed Partido Komunista ng Pilipinas. Originally, the CPP relied on modest Chinese aid. The funds ceased in 1975, but the CPP, by this time a powerful endogenous force, went from strength to strength. By the mid-1980s, the New People's Army had more than 15,000 guerrilla fighters and was operating in the majority of the country's 73 provinces, mainly in the countryside but also in some cities, such as Davao in Mindanao. When they deemed it necessary, the Communists used ruthless techniques to gain ascendancy. They shot local mayors and heads of villages to terrorize the people and weaken the local administration.

One of the few moderating influences on the political scene was the Catholic Church. Cardinal Jaime Sin, the archbishop of Manila, offered constructive criticism of the Marcos regime, although not to the point of encouraging the extreme left. The Church was split between those who backed Marcos and the majority, who followed the Cardinal's middle way. There was also a handful, perhaps 1 percent, who supported the Communists and even worked with them.

Political passions in the islands of the Philippines were already running high when canvassing for the 1986 presidential elections began. In the course of a campaign marred by bloodshed and murder, Marcos's supporters subjected the electoral process to every kind of abuse—from vote-buying to the theft of ballot boxes. Eventually, Marcos proclaimed himself the winner, with 53 percent of the vote. The opposition, led by Corazón Aquino, widow of the murdered Benigno Aquino, contested the result with massive, nonviolent demonstrations.

Two weeks after the election charade, a group of army officers, headed by Defense Minister Juan Ponce Enrile, proclaimed open revolt against the Marcos regime. Thousands of Manila's citizens thronged the road to the rebels' camp and prevented government troops from reaching it. As Marcos's position became untenable, Corazón Aquino was sworn in as the Philippines' new president. Twelve hours later, Marcos was persuaded to leave the country. No sooner had he gone than Aquino opened his opulent Manila palace to the public so that Filipinos could judge the outrageously extravagant life-style of the autocrat who had ruled them for 21 years. They came by the thousands to gape at the lofty rooms and old master paintings—not to mention Imelda Marcos's gold washbasin and 1,060 pairs of shoes.

Mrs. Aquino drew support from all over the Philippines, but nowhere was the commitment stronger than in Manila, where every class, from the business elite to the poorest of the poor, had glimpsed the excesses of its former leader and his family. It was the people of Manila who were at the heart of the struggle to oust Marcos, and it was they who rejoiced most ecstatically at the change of rule.

Manila habitually sets the course for the rest of the country. It is not only the hub of Filipino politics but the base of the country's economy, religion, entertainment, and communications. The city is the home of two thirds of the Philippines' industries, and its harbor is the scene of a constant coming and going of cargo vessels from ports all over the world. Every year, Manila draws hundreds of thousands of newcomers, who add to its already immense population and its social problems. In 1903, Manila had a population of 220,000; modern Metro Manila, the term used to describe the conurbation that now links 13 suburban cities and towns with the Manila of old, has seven million inhabitants and is still growing fast. Its downtown area is full of reminders of the past—old Spanish forts, a Christian churchyard guarded by Chinese lions—yet the present intrudes everywhere. Like all great Asian cities, Manila is intensely dynamic, noisy, overcrowded, and snarled in endless traffic jams, whose most eye-catching constituents are jeepneys—gaudily decorated trucks converted into the bus-cum-taxis that have become the unofficial emblem of the place.

Metro Manila has more than 100 movie theaters, and there is a thriving and sometimes innovative Philippine film industry. Another of Manila's addictions is the Basque sport of jai alai, one of the heritages of Spanish rule. The action is something like squash, except that players wield crescent-shaped wicker baskets instead of rackets. Spectators place bets on the outcome of this, the fastest of ball games.

For people with money to spend, there are avenues lined with restaurants famous for some of the finest cooking in the East, and nightclubs where Filipino jazz musicians uphold their reputation as the best in Asia. There is also a variety of pleasure dens and massage parlors where one can form relationships that, as one guidebook delicately phrases it, are "intensified by their briefness and generally monetary nature."

Not far from the glamorous boulevards of affluent Manila lies a very different world—the twisted alleys of Tondo, where some 250,000 squatters live jammed together in tin-roofed shanties. With virtually no plumbing, the stench is appalling, but television antennas rise high above many of the ramshackle dwellings to proclaim to the world that things are looking up. Many people manage to live an honest and quasi-normal life in these squalid surroundings, perhaps picking rags and scrap metal from the city's trash dumps; some people, however, resort to prostitution and crime. Manila's slums are dangerous places, where outsiders only venture in broad daylight and in groups of three or more. The litter-strewn Tondo alleys make a perfect hideout for fugitives, racketeers, and malefactors.

Those who have turned to petty thievery to rise above the anonymous poverty of the slums sometimes move on to grand larceny as a respectable way of life. Manila has long been a violent place, and its organized-crime gangs are reminiscent of Chicago's in the Al Capone era; there is said to be a murder every hour.

The peasant life the Tondo squatters left behind begins only a short distance from the outskirts of the capital. Villages are mostly unplanned agglomerations of one- and two-story frame houses, some with corrugated-tin roofs and others with palm thatch. A good part of everyday life is lived in perpetually green gardens wreathed with vines and flowers, or on a sandy patch by the sea.

If the village is large enough to warrant a town hall, a school, or a hospital,

it may also have a public park adorned with a statue of the scholarly revolutionary José Rizal, bending over his writing table with a kerosene lamp at his side. Nearby there will be restaurants and cafés where people spend their free time sitting under awnings, sipping soft drinks, and talking volubly: Filipinos have a lot to say to one another, even if they have been neighbors for 20 years. If there is a bus stop nearby, each bus will be greeted by girls offering bananas or oranges or homemade sweets to passengers through the open windows; competition is fierce but good-natured.

For most rural families, the income from such commerce is a sideline to farming or fishing. On many of the smaller islands, where space is scarce, the land is divided into peasant farms, each growing a variety of crops. The bulk of the Philippines' rice comes

from the largest island, Luzon, whose extensive central lowlands permit large-scale agriculture.

Most of the sugar plantations in the Philippines are concentrated on the fourth-largest island, Negros. Until the 19th century, Negros was almost uninhabited, but by 1893, it harbored 274 steam-operated sugar mills, with hundreds of thousands of acres of sugar-cane fields to supply them and a vast population of agricultural workers who had immigrated from nearby islands. For decades, the sugar industry provided a livelihood directly or indirectly for about five million people, but the decline in world sugar prices in the 1980s bankrupted many plantations. Few of the unemployed field hands have found alternative work; they face the choice between the squalor of a city slum and a life of desperate poverty in the lush green countryside. Eventually,

5

some may be rescued by tourism, for Negros, seen from afar, is a Hollywood stereotype of an island paradise. Its purple mountains are capped with white clouds and descend to superb beaches and underwater gardens of coral reefs; hot springs and waterfalls abound in its forests.

Some Philippine islands have already adapted themselves to the tourist economy. In parts of Cebu and Panay, for example, villages of *nipah* huts—a palm-thatch and bamboo version of a motel cabin—have sprung up to accommodate the Swiss, Australians, and Californians who represent the leading edge of the tourist invasion. Hotels and beach clubs have also proliferated, and

in some places, only the elderly are left working the land, while all the young people are busy as waiters, masseurs, or peddlers of coral necklaces.

Still, there are communities in the Philippines that have not yet succumbed to the blandishments of modernism. The 1.5 million Muslims of western Mindanao, Palawan, and the Sulu Archipelago constitute a prime example of a fiercely independent people still clinging to the traditions they inherited from their ancestors. Other Filipinos call them Moros. The word is a misnomer bestowed by the early Spanish colonizers, who had just finished driving the Moors from Spain and to whom all Muslims were *moros*.

Ethnically, the Philippine Muslims are scarcely less Malay than the rest of the islands' population, although their aquiline noses suggest an admixture of Arab stock. Ideologically, however, they are a race apart. They have never been reconciled to any central government, and in the 1970s, they began a simmering guerrilla war against the republic's authority. In 1976, the Philippine government agreed in principle to grant the Moros considerable regional autonomy, including their own judiciary, legislature, and security force. So far, however, little of substance has been devolved.

The Moros have the most striking dress of the Philippines: The men wear

sarongs with braided waistcoats and wide cummerbunds, topped with a fez or a turban; many are armed with a more-than-decorative dagger. The women wear trousers with sarilike robes or brocade jackets whose golden threads and shining buttons sparkle in the sunlight.

The Moros live in hierarchic communities under sultans and *datus* who also administer the religious courts known as *agama*. They practice polygamy, which is technically illegal but is tolerated by the government, and they observe the Koranic law by which a man can repudiate a wife whenever he wishes. Yet women are much freer to come and go as they please than women in

most other Islamic societies, and the literacy rate is as high among Moro women as among Moro men.

The Muslim coastal tribes—Samal, Yakan, and Tausug—make their living from the sea, mainly as fishermen but also as interisland traders, and occasionally as smugglers and pirates. The southernmost islands of the Sulu Archipelago are considered bandit country and no-go areas for outsiders without the proper introductions. The Samal travel for hundreds of miles in homemade boats that are often only hollowed-out logs buoyed by twin outriggers and fitted with a single sail. During World War II, an outrigger manned by escaping Samals and Americans made the 3,125-mile crossing to Australia under sail.

The Filipinos with the closest ties to the sea, however, are the Bajau Laut—a group of no more than 20,000 to 30,000, many of whom spend all their lives on small houseboats. The whole of their sea-gypsy existence is governed by the tides. When typhoons lash the islands, they ride out the storms aboard their boats rather than trying to seek safety on land: Terra firma makes them feel "landsick." Children are born, love affairs are consummated, and marriages are celebrated aboard the boats. Hardly touched by the modern world, the Bajau Laut rarely know how old they are or what year it is.

Other Filipinos might envy the detachment of the Bajau Laut. Most of the islanders—citydwellers and country-folk alike—have been unable to escape the momentous upheavals that have buffeted their country in recent years. The martial law of the 1970s, the economic crisis of the mid-1980s, Marcos's sudden departure in 1986, generated

Against a backdrop of high-rise hotels lining a waterfront boulevard, pleasure craft are moored in the Manila Yacht Club marina. The building in the foreground was built for the 1974 Miss Universe contest; it now serves as a theater and cultural center.

waves that reached almost every corner. Communist insurgency has represented a far more serious threat to the status quo here than in other ASEAN countries. Elsewhere, communism has normally been associated with ethnic minorities—such as the Chinese in Malaysia—or has been bolstered from outside. But under Marcos's repressive yoke, Filipino communism burgeoned as a native movement with growing popular support.

Even if democracy in the post-Marcos era succeeds in quelling extremism, the reconstruction of Filipino society is bound to be a long and painful task. Under 21 years of Marcos's rule, every institution from village headships to the supreme court was filled from the ranks of Marcos cronies. Until the institutions are again representative and viable, the Philippines is unlikely to find the will to radically tackle economic and social problems.

The other members of ASEAN are nervously watching their volatile neighbor. During Marcos's last years in power, the Philippines came to be seen as the odd man out in the group, and the other heads of state avoided Manila. While taking advantage of the economic weakness of the Philippines to expand their own trade, its partners feared contagion with the Communist insurgency. The more authoritarian among them were disconcerted by the popular movement that swept Corazón Aquino to power. Indonesia and Malaysia, intent on keeping religion out of politics, looked askance at the Church's prominent political role. If the Philippines succeeds in regaining its equilibrium, its neighbors will be greatly relieved to find that ASEAN's most serious internal threat to stability has at last been overcome. □

AMPHIBIOUS LIVING
IN A REMOTE ARCHIPELAGO

Many of the denizens of the Sulu Archipelago in the southernmost Philippines are more at home on the sea than on land. The Samal, a group of Islamic farmers and seafarers, build stilt villages in the shallows around the islands' shores. The watery expanses surrounding their homes afford some protection against intruders in an area notorious for lawlessness.

Scattered among the Samal colonies, the autonomous Bajau Laut have taken amphibious existence one step further; some of them spend their entire lives afloat, roaming the coasts in small houseboats. The boat dwellers depend on fishing and a modicum of trade with the Samal for their livelihood. These sea-gypsies have been the poorest of the archipelago's peoples for generations; their waterborne homes are picturesque but primitive, providing cramped and uncomfortable living quarters. Traditionally disdained by their neighbors, many Bajau Laut have recently begun to build stilt houses, hoping that a settled home will be the key to higher status.

A Bajau Laut family sets out on a fishing expedition in the houseboat that serves as their permanent home. Its roof of wood and plastic scraps shelters about 20 square feet of living space in which adults and children alike must eat, work, and sleep.

In a stilt village near Zamboanga, a town on the westernmost tip of Mindanao, a Samal man relaxes on his porch. Every day, the ebbing tide flushes away household sewage and the incoming tide brings fresh fish almost to his door.

A settlement near Sitangkai at the archipelago's southern tip provides shelter and mooring space for a community of Bajau Laut. The houses perch above a submerged coral reef one and a quarter miles offshore.

At high tide, boats provide the only links between houses in Sitangkai, inhabited mainly by Bajau Laut.

On the porch of her one-room home, a Samal woman does laundry as her daughter prepares vegetables. A straw mat shelters them from the sun.

Samal women set up a vegetable stand on a meandering bridge that connects the land and sea villages of Rio Hondo, near Zamboanga.

In the metal light of dawn, an outrigger glides into Zamboanga harbor with a cargo of helmet shells destined to catch the eye of tourists. Boats such as these, the workhorses of the Samal, can reach speeds of more than 11 knots when the wind is up.

Smiling figures and miniature water-craft mark Bajau Laut graves on the island of Great Santa Cruz, near Zamboanga, used as a cemetery by the boat dwellers. Except for visits to the market, the Bajau Laut are brought ashore only by death.

Workers balancing themselves on bamboo scaffolding restore a gilded roof at Wat Phra Keo, Thailand's most magnificent Buddhist temple complex. The ornate buildings, glittering with glass mosaics and Chinese ceramics, stand within the walls of the royal palace in Bangkok.

AN UNCONQUERED KINGDOM

Geography sets Thailand apart from the other members of ASEAN. Located on the Asian mainland, the country largely escaped the main historic seaborne influences—notably the Muslim religion and European rule—that shaped the maritime world to the south and east. But Thailand has been far closer than the other ASEAN states to the succession of crises that have plagued Indochina in the decades following World War II. Since the invasion of Kampuchea in 1979 by Vietnam, Thailand's old rival, Thailand has been the only ASEAN state directly confronting an expansionist Communist power across its national border.

Thailand has strong cultural affinities with its mainland neighbors. Like the people of Burma, Kampuchea, Laos, and parts of southern China, the Thais are Buddhists of the Theravada orthodoxy—the form of the religion closest to Buddha's teachings. Offering a liberating "middle path" between extremes of reason and passion, asceticism and sensuality, Theravada Buddhism has shaped the Thais into a people who eschew extremism and fundamentalism. Foreign visitors to Thailand invariably note with delight the grace and decorum of the people, their sense of fun, and their concern for the well-being of others. Buddhist lessons of correct action and speech, of nonviolence and loving-kindness, have greatly contributed to such traits.

Although they share a Buddhist culture with their neighbors, Thais are acutely aware of a history that they feel makes them unique. There has been a major Thai state in the present territory of Thailand since the 14th century, and the country is one of the few in Asia to have escaped Western colonialism. The monarchy is a potent symbol of the country's historical continuity and a focus for celebrations of nationhood. In 1982, there was a magnificent commemoration of the 200th anniversary of the founding of Bangkok and the Chakri dynasty, of which King Bhumibol Adulyadej is the ninth monarch in direct succession.

Devotion to the monarchy, to Buddhism, and to the idea of the nation creates a distinctive Thai identity that is strengthened by a cultural uniformity more marked than in the other large members of ASEAN. The country does not have the multiplicity of languages found in Indonesia and the Philippines, or as complex an ethnic mixture as Malaysia. Thai is the first language of at least 85 percent of the population of 50 million, and it is understood by almost everyone. Thai is one of a large cluster of languages that are spoken in all bordering countries as well as in southern China and northern Vietnam. Unlike Malay, these languages are monosyllabic and tonal.

For all their similarities, the Thais are not quite the single harmonious family that they seem at first glance. They fall into several groups that speak different dialects of Thai and have their own traditions of folklore and music. The four main groups—the inhabitants of the central plain, the southerners, the northerners, and the northeasterners—correspond to the main geographic divisions of the country, which did not come under centralized rule until late in the last century.

Thailand's great central plain was once forested but now consists of unbroken paddy fields. It is the most fertile part of the country, and it grows the bulk of Thailand's rice. For much of its history, the capital of the independent kingdom of Thailand has been located on the central plain and the people in this region have been the dominant group in the country.

The long neck of land to the south that links central Thailand with Malaysia is somewhat less fertile than the central plain. For the past century, it has been a rubber-producing area. The people of the region have long been ruled by the central Thais, and although their dialect sets them apart, most of them have a life-style quite similar to those of other regions.

North and west of the central plain, the land rises to forested mountains. Rice is also grown here, as are such temperate crops as corn. Until the late 19th century, the northern Thais belonged to a semi-independent kingdom that paid tribute to the central Thai kingdom but conducted its own affairs.

The vast northeastern region, separated from Laos by the meandering Mekong River, is a high plateau cursed with infertile soil and low rainfall. This area is the poorest in Thailand: About seven million people in the northeast are officially categorized as living in poverty. Like the north, this region had a history of semiautonomy until the late

A neon sign cryptically advertises a restaurant on one of Bangkok's main streets. The capital city offers some of the most varied night life in the world, ranging from the refined to the salacious—from folk dramas and musical evenings to bars, discotheques, and massage parlors.

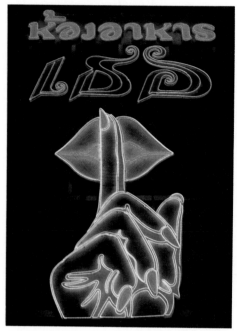

19th century: The people speak the same language as the Laotians across the border, and they have at times been linked politically with Lao kingdoms.

In the outlying regions and especially the northeast, many people feel that they have been neglected and disregarded by the national government. But the central Thai ascendancy plays down regional loyalties and discontents: Its version of the language is taught in schools throughout the country, and the unity of the nation is constantly proclaimed in government publications and school textbooks.

The concept of unity must accommodate not only the Thai populations but the 15 percent who are not Thai. Chinese make up the largest ethnic minority with about four million people, or 8 percent of the population. Chinese began arriving in Thailand in the late 19th and early 20th centuries, and they

The illuminations of the Royal Orchid Sheraton Hotel are reflected in the surface of Bangkok's Chao Phraya River. With more than two million visitors a year, Thailand's tourist industry ranks with rice as the highest foreign-exchange earner.

have long dominated Thai business.

The Chinese in Thailand are assimilated to a far greater degree than they are in either Islamic Malaysia or Indonesia. Dietary restrictions do not hinder social life: The Thais, unlike other Muslim peoples, eat pork. There are no barriers to intermarriage, which has occurred at all social levels in Thailand—from the peasantry to the royal family. Moreover, the Chinese are happy to embrace Thailand's Buddhism.

The next largest minority consists of people of Malay ancestry who practice the Muslim faith—although they live otherwise in very much the same way as the Thais. They account for about 3 percent of the population and are largely concentrated in four provinces close to the Malaysian border.

There is a third broad category of peoples of non-Thai origin, numbering considerably fewer than one million, who mainly inhabit the hills and forest areas of the north. They include the Akha, Hmong, Karen, Khmu, Lahu, Lawa, Lisu, Yao, and Lao. Some, such as the Lawa, have been in Thailand as long as the Thais, while others have arrived in this century. Most are animists, but some have been converted to Christianity or Buddhism. Most practice shifting rice cultivation out of necessity; many would become wet-rice farmers like their Thai neighbors if there were suitable land. Until recently, the hill peoples were scarcely noticed by their compatriots. Even now, they are somewhat grudgingly accepted, and some have not yet been granted citizenship. Most are very poor.

The one source of money traditionally available to the hill peoples has been opium. The poppies are grown throughout the Golden Triangle—the notorious stretch of land where Thai-

land, Burma, and Laos meet. In addition to producing some of the opium itself, Thailand has been the major conduit to the West for Burmese opium. In the early 1970s, the United States, alarmed at its soaring addiction rates, put pressure on Thailand to suppress the drug. The Thais toughened their legislation against producers and transporters of narcotics and stepped up surveillance. The measures had little effect for several years, mainly because many government officials had a corrupt interest in the trade. In recent years, however, both trafficking and internal production have declined, and some efforts have been made to find alternative cash crops, such as tea and tobacco, for the hill peoples.

The non-Thais living in Thailand also include some Vietnamese, who settled in the northeast in the 1940s and 1950s to escape the fighting against the French in their own country, and hundreds of thousands of Kampucheans, many of whom flooded across the Kampuchea-Thai border as refugees after the 1979 Vietnamese invasion of Kampuchea. The host country has generally pursued a humane attitude toward the refugees, but they remain in camps along the border and are not assimilated into the mainstream.

The Thais themselves arrived in their land since written history. Speakers of Thai and its related languages probably originated in the southern and southwestern parts of what is now China. During the first 1,000 years A.D., they spread in a southerly direction along river valleys as far as northern Burma and Assam to the southwest, and northern Laos and Vietnam to the southeast.

Wherever they stopped, they coexisted for long periods with other ethnic groups. They paid tribute to powerful states such as the Mon kingdoms of Burma and northern Thailand and the Khmer Empire in Cambodia. These states were already strongly influenced by both Buddhism and Hinduism. Eventually the Thais, too, embraced the Buddhist religion and many Hindu customs. They practiced irrigated rice cultivation, and where they had some autonomy, they organized themselves into loose federations of small local territories—often single valleys, each controlled by a chief.

These federations worked well when the Thais inhabited mountainous terrain where communication was difficult. But as they edged southward into the flatter expanses of Thailand, centralized political systems became more practical. By the 13th century, several small Thai states had emerged. A kingdom based in Sukhothai, at the north-

6

ern end of the central plain, was the earliest; another kingdom, which was based in Chiang Mai in the north, followed soon after.

The greatest of the early Thai states was the kingdom of Ayutthaya, founded in 1351 as the Khmer Empire was waning. It was known as Siam by the Khmer, Europeans, and other outsiders. From its eponymous capital on the Thai central plain, Ayutthaya claimed suzerainty over all the territory of present-day Thailand, as well as parts of what are now Malaya, Burma, Kampuchea, southern China, and Laos. The other Thai kingdoms were to varying degrees vassals of Ayutthaya. In its turn, Ayutthaya paid tribute to the em-

peror of China. Ayutthaya was to retain its dominance for more than 400 years.

The Ayutthaya kingdom developed ideas about the exercise of power that are echoed to this day in state rituals and the popular imagination. The king both represented and sought to maintain a symbolic harmony of earthly and cosmic forces. At times, he was referred to as a future Buddha or, in a more Hindu idiom, as a god-king.

The social and political order was symbolically constructed as a model of the Hindu-Buddhist universe. The king on his throne was identified with the Hindu god Indra, who ruled one of the heavens from the top of Mount Meru, the cosmological center of the

world. The royal capital had three concentric moats and ramparts representing the three seas surrounding Mount Meru. A hierarchy of princes and officials mirrored the retinue of lords serving Indra.

Elaborate trappings emphasized each functionary's place in the hierarchy. The king, for example, was on state occasions surmounted by nine tiers of umbrellas, equivalent to the crowns of European rulers; the rulers of the tributary states were accorded umbrellas of lesser scale. The senior officials were given a set of symbolic objects denoting their rank, which included cushions, seals, utensils for preparing betel nut—a mild narcotic—and

132

spittoons for disposing of their betel-stained saliva. And, on appointment, each official was also given a new name.

Nowadays, the nine umbrellas still form part of the king's regalia, and every government employee, even primary schoolteachers, wears a uniform with a grade proclaimed on the shoulder. The display of rank has become ingrained in Thai society.

The Ayutthaya kings devised enduring strategies for maintaining a more-than-symbolic hold on power. One of them was centralization. Independent local princes were converted whenever possible into court functionaries and were thus detached from their natural constituency of support. There was no separate military: All officials were supposed to raise armies, and manpower was used for civil or military purposes according to need.

Even the Buddhist order of monks was co-opted to provide the state with moral legitimacy and a means of controlling its subjects. Monasteries established throughout the kingdom helped to assert the presence of the state. The monkhood was generally flexible and prepared to accommodate the political order for the sake of securing the adherence of rulers to Buddhist values. Little has changed in these respects. There is still considerable overlap between secular and religious life.

What has changed profoundly is the economic basis of the state. The material power of the Ayutthaya kingdom rested on the conscripted or enslaved labor of the people and on a system of royal trade-monopolies. Everyone in the population other than the king, who was above rank, was given a number that indicated entitlements as well as obligations toward superiors. The highest-ranking individual below the king was the viceroy, with 100,000 points. Other nobles appointed by the king had between 400 and 99,999 points. Most citizens, with 25 points or fewer, labored either directly for the king or for the small class of officials and aristocrats. Beggars and slaves received five points. The fact that they were designated any points at all indicates that they had some rights, notably recourse to justice.

European contact with the Ayutthaya kingdom began in the 16th century. The Portuguese sent an envoy in 1509 and were soon providing training in musketry and gunnery. The Dutch followed the Portuguese, and in 1609, a Siamese mission was received at The Hague. In 1612, British traders took a respectful letter from King James I to the Siamese king and reported back that the city of Ayutthaya was as large and impressive as London. For much of the 17th century, Europeans were granted rights to trade with Ayutthaya. But the Siamese, rightly, suspected the Europeans of imperial and missionary ambitions and terminated relations in the late 17th century. Apart from a few isolated visits, links with Europe were severed until well into the 19th century. Ayutthaya remained a cosmopolitan city nonetheless, with a substantial Chinese population, a corps of Japanese guards, and many Turkish, Arabic, and Persian traders.

In 1767, a Burmese army defeated the kingdom and sacked and burned the capital. The Siamese rallied soon after this disaster, ousting the Burmese and reestablishing their realm. Instead of rebuilding the city, they founded a new capital farther south at Thonburi, then moved it to nearby Bangkok in 1782. The territory of the kingdom was expanded and commerce encouraged.

During the reigns of King Mongkut (1851-1868) and his son, King Chulalongkorn (1868-1910), change accelerated. Mongkut was the model for the larger-than-life monarch in the Rodgers and Hammerstein musical *The King and I*, which was based on the memoirs of the British governess employed to educate some of the king's 82 children. The show caricatured Mongkut as a capricious Oriental tyrant; in reality, his harem notwithstanding, he was a highly educated and sophisticated man. He and his son Chulalongkorn directed the country on the one hand toward modernization and reform, which were to forestall European empire builders in their search for territory, and on the other hand toward increasing state absolutism.

Forced labor and debt bondage were gradually eliminated; slavery was completely abolished in 1905. The country's infrastructure was developed: Thousands of Chinese arrived annually to be employed as laborers, building canals, ports, and—later—railroads. Meanwhile, the monarchs strengthened their positions by appointing brothers and other relatives as ministers and regional governors in place of the provincial aristocracy. These developments were generally encouraged and supported by Western countries, which began to show a new interest in relations with Siam.

In 1855, Sir John Bowring, British governor of Hong Kong, negotiated a treaty with King Mongkut, who soon signed similar agreements with other industrializing countries in Europe. These pacts allowed Westerners valuable economic and legal privileges. The king gave up his monopoly on trade, and importers had to pay a tax of only 3 percent of their goods' value; imports

On the outskirts of Mae Hong Son, a village of 6,000 people in northwestern Thailand, a Buddhist temple compound nestles in a forest enclave. Although the temple is the spiritual heart of most Thai communities, it is usually built in a secluded quarter.

133

6

of opium and bullion were duty free. The British wanted to buy rice to feed the immigrant workers in Malaya, and the Thai people were encouraged to cultivate new land as they emerged from forced labor and slavery. King Chulalongkorn invited Westerners to act as ministerial advisers. He sent his sons to be educated in Berlin, London, and St. Petersburg.

Thanks in no small part to its rulers' astuteness, Siam remained sovereign over its core territory. But the British and the French were consolidating their positions in Southeast Asia, and they coveted many of Siam's outlying regions. The country had to accept considerable losses of territory to colonial Burma, Cambodia, Laos, and Malaya. And the British, holding key financial advisory posts, dominated Siam's economy until World War II.

The effort to build a modern Siamese state faltered for a while after the death of King Chulalongkorn in 1910, but King Prajadhipok, who ascended the throne in 1925, was a reformer anxious to share decision making with his ministers. He even considered giving the country a constitution, but his min-

isters opposed him. Some of his younger, Western-educated officials, however, were less eager to abandon the idea and thought the time was ripe for such a change. In 1932, a group of civil servants and army officers engineered a bloodless coup that swept away the senior ministers and put an end to absolute monarchy. It was not directed against the king himself, who was kept on as constitutional head of state.

The new young leaders of Siam were the first generation outside the royal family to be educated abroad and instilled with Western ideas. The civilian element included men of socialist leanings, among them Pridi Phanomyong, who was later to become regent. But the military predominated. Nationalism was in the air, and the army seemed the natural successor to absolute monarchy; besides, the army was better equipped and better organized than any other Thai institution.

The military has dominated Thai politics during most of the intervening decades, setting a pattern of authoritarian rule that is still evident to some extent. Thailand, however, has escaped

the extremes suffered under most military regimes. Because the country's rulers have been able to rely on the traditional loyalty and obedience of the people, they have usually achieved the control they desired by using comparatively limited measures of violence and intimidation.

Nationalist sentiments dominated the first years of constitutional monarchy. Direct state involvement in industrial and commercial enterprises was encouraged, and the Chinese suffered legal discrimination. In 1939, Siam was renamed Thailand in accordance with the patriotic enthusiasms of the time. The nationalists were attracted by European and Japanese fascist models; their expansionist rhetoric found expression in a short war against the French in Laos and Cambodia during 1940 and 1941.

At the end of 1941, the Japanese, en route to attack the British in Burma and Malaya, demanded access through Thailand by air, land, and sea. Thailand resisted for less than a day, then opted for self-preservation. The prime minister allowed the Japanese forces military rights of passage in return for assurances of respect for national independence. But many Thai leaders, including Pridi and the ambassador to the United States, Seni Pramoj, resisted the Japanese ascendency. When Thailand's ruling regime declared war on Britain and the United States in 1942, Seni Pramoj refused to deliver the declaration to the U.S. government.

A "Free Thai" anti-Japanese movement was formed in 1944. The war ended before the movement could make a substantial contribution to the Allies' cause, but its endeavors meant that Thailand was spared the full disadvantages of being a hostile nation. In

A 19th-century mural depicts a scene from the Ramakien, the Thai version of the Indian Ramayana epic. In this episode, the white monkey-general Hanuman inflates his body into a living bridge to allow the army of the hero Rama to cross a river.

A CHRONOLOGY OF KEY EVENTS

c. 600-900 A.D. Mon people originating in west China form kingdoms in Thailand. Missionaries from Ceylon convert the Mon to Buddhism. Thai people from southern China begin to move southward; some settle among the Mon in Thailand and form small states.

c. 900-1300 The Khmer, related to the Mon, rule a Cambodian-based empire that extends over most of present-day Thailand. Mon rulers introduce the Khmer and Thai peoples to Buddhist influences.

1238 Thai chieftains in the northern part of Thailand's central plain defeat their Khmer overlords and found the first independent Thai kingdom of Sukhothai.

1350-1767 As Sukhothai declines, a new Thai kingdom based at Ayutthaya, in the south, rises to prominence. In this rich state, architecture, bronze sculpture (below), and literature all reach new heights.

1509 The Portuguese send an ambassador to Ayutthaya, initiating nearly two centuries of contact with Europe.

1688 General Phra Phetracha, suspicious of the French missionaries and ambassadors welcomed by the king, stages a coup and inaugurates a 150-year period of Thai isolation from the West.

1767-1782 A Burmese army levels the city of Ayutthaya. Taksin, a brilliant Thai general, drives out the Burmese. Assuming the royal title, he founds a new capital at Thonburi, near modern Bangkok.

1782-1809 General Chakkri leads a coup, founding the present Thai royal house. He moves the capital to Bangkok.

1851-1868 The scholar-king, Mongkut (above, right), ends the policy of isolation,

signing treaties of friendship and commerce with several Western powers. His country, now known as Siam, quickly becomes a major exporter of rice.

1868-1910 King Chulalongkorn modernizes Siam rapidly. He abolishes slavery, founds schools, encourages study abroad, and builds railways and roads.

1932 A military and civilian group mounts a bloodless coup against absolute monarchy. The king remains as a constitutional symbol.

1939 Siam is renamed Thailand.

1941-1945 During World War II, Thailand allows access to Japanese troops to invade Burma and Malaya. In 1942, Thailand declares war on Britain and the United States. However, the Free Thai Movement contributes notably to Allied efforts to resist the Japanese.

1946 Thailand joins the United Nations.

1947 The army takes over the government. It rules for most of the next few decades, allowing varying degrees of civilian participation.

1965-1976 Supporting American action in Vietnam, Thailand plays host to large numbers of troops and aircraft.

1973 Student demonstrations in Bangkok bring down the military government, inaugurating three years of civilian democratic rule.

1976 A coup reinstates the army to power; remaining U.S. military units depart.

1981 The Prem government survives a coup; Communist insurgency collapses.

1985 Loyalists in Bangkok defeat a second military coup attempt.

1946, it became one of the first Asian countries to join the UN.

After a brief postwar period of civilian government and a flowering of democratic and trade-union freedoms, the military regained its dominant position. The army and the police (who in Thailand are equipped with tanks, aircraft, and heavy weapons) were greatly strengthened in the 1950s by American military aid. Thai governments began to ally themselves enthusiastically with the United States and to take up the vehemently anti-Communist position they still maintain. Thai soldiers fought in the Korean War in the 1950s and later saw action in Vietnam. The headquarters of the anti-Communist Southeast Asia Treaty Organization (SEATO) was first established in Bangkok in 1954.

Senior military and police officials were not only interested in politics and warfare. They also established themselves on the boards of innumerable financial and commercial companies and grew rich through illegal and corrupt economic practices. One notorious police chief, General Phao, made his fortune in the opium trade; General Sarit Thanarat, the future prime minister, became wealthy by diverting funds from the Lottery Bureau.

Sarit seized power in a bloodless coup d'etat in 1957. Despite his personal venality, his six-year period of power laid the groundwork for much of the economic growth that has since occurred in Thailand, keeping its per capita income well ahead of that of Indonesia, though not as high as Malaysia's. At the World Bank's urging, new policies were introduced in Thailand's first Five Year National Development Plan, launched in 1961. Direct state involvement in the economy decreased, and private and

6

foreign investment were promoted. The government spent heavily on infrastructure such as roads and electric power, urban development, and education. After Sarit's death, the boom continued, providing an average 8.6 percent growth rate for the 1960s, nearly double that of the 1950s.

The fastest expansion was seen in the manufacturing, service, and mining sectors. Thailand is estimated to have 12 percent of the world's reserves of tin, and tin production made a sizable contribution to export earnings. Thailand has been the world's largest producer of rubies and sapphires since the early 1970s. Manufacturing focused at first on replacing basics, such as cement, with domestic products and on creating consumer goods for the home market, such as textiles, beer, and soft drinks. Much wealth became concentrated in a few large conglomerates, but small family firms employing up to 10 people were—and remain—a feature of the Thai economy.

Agriculture declined in importance relative to manufacturing; its contribution to the national economy was to shrink from more than 50 percent in the late 1950s to less than 20 percent in the 1980s. Agricultural production was still expanding, however. Despite a fast-growing population, Thailand's peasant farmers continued to produce enough rice to feed their compatriots and leave a surplus for export. In the late 1980s, Thailand was the world's fifth-largest producer of rice and the largest exporter of the commodity.

In the 1960s, many farmers moved away from an exclusive concentration on the national staple. They began growing other export crops, including corn, tapioca, sugarcane, pineapple, and tobacco. In the late 1980s, these products were Thailand's principal exports after rice, rubber, and tin.

Although he was authoritarian and outlawed opposition to his regime, Sarit won popularity through his economic achievements. He was also astute enough to enhance his own legitimacy by harnessing both religion and the monarchy. A series of laws organized the *sangha,* the order of Buddhist monks, into a multilayered hierarchy in which each level had direct links with a corresponding level of civil government. Although the structure gave the government tighter control over religious affairs, the monks were acquiescent. Some monks became involved in government programs and went on missions among the hill peoples to convert them to Buddhism and elicit their loyalty to the state.

Meanwhile, the king assumed a more public role than had been customary since 1932; all the ritual of old reappeared. Although the Thais no longer thought of their rulers as divine, they continued to regard them with a profound respect and affection.

After Sarit's death in 1963, American presence and influence continued to grow. Many military bases were built around the country, and much of the air war against Vietnam and Laos was conducted from them. In addition, hundreds of thousands of American military personnel passed through Thailand for "rest and recreation."

American military expenditure helped to create an economic boom. Meanwhile, Japan began to invest in Thailand and soon became its largest trading partner. Banks and luxury hotels proliferated; new industries were established; eight-lane bypasses were built around Bangkok, and "strategic highways" linked the regions with the rapidly expanding capital.

But not everybody profited from the economic growth of the period. Peasants were among the worst off. The expansion of agricultural production had been achieved largely by putting virgin land under the plow. Techniques were still labor intensive, and farmers had not benefited from even a modest version of the Green Revolution that had brought prosperity to other ASEAN nations. Although much of the central plain was irrigated, there were few large-scale projects elsewhere in the country.

In the late 1960s, poor farmers, particularly in the north, the northeast,

Vendors display plump produce at a floating market in Damnoen Saduak, a town southwest of Bangkok. Canals used to be central Thailand's main arteries; even today, the country's 1,000 miles of waterways remain vital for transportation and trade.

6

and the south, grew increasingly resentful of the government's lack of commitment to rural development. In their frustration, the disadvantaged farmers were attracted for a time to the Communist party of Thailand. Founded in 1942, the party had for most of the intervening years been banned and obliged to operate clandestinely. In 1965, it began to put into effect a policy of armed insurrection.

Ignoring the predicament of the farmers, the Thai government reacted vigorously to the symptoms of their alienation. Within only a few years, most of Thailand's 75 provinces were declared zones of Communist infiltration. Counterinsurgency now became the watchword, and even the monks were strongly encouraged to give anti-Communist sermons.

The universities became another focus of discontent. Many students had become critical of foreign economic and cultural influences and began to be aware of the conditions of urban and rural workers, with whom they were coming in contact for the first time.

A movement for the reinstatement and reform of the Constitution, which had been abrogated after a coup in 1971, attracted widespread support. In October 1973, there were massive demonstrations on the streets of Bangkok. Government troops opened fire on the crowds—an action without precedent in the country's history—and scores of protestors were killed. The king acted immediately to prevent further bloodshed. Deprived of his support, the two leading military men in the government had to leave the country.

With their departure, a long period of authoritarian rule came to an end, and a series of civilian governments followed. New political parties campaigned openly, progressive journals multiplied, left-wing students made their voices heard. Parliament, responding to popular wishes, introduced legislation on agricultural rent for the minority of peasants who were not freeholders.

A radical realignment of foreign policy took place, reflecting not only the climate within Thailand but a new external reality. The Vietnam War had ended, and Communist governments now ruled Laos, the Khmer Republic (Cambodia), and Vietnam. The Thais recognized that they would do well to

be on reasonable terms with their Communist neighbors, however distasteful their regimes. Seeking connections with the nearest superpower that might support them against Vietnamese aggression, Thailand opened diplomatic relations with China in 1975. Responding to left-wing demands and also realizing that relations with Vietnam would be easier if links with the United States were loosened, the Thai government asked the Americans to close down their military bases in the country. The Americans, disillusioned by the Vietnam War and in any case well ensconced in the Philippines, agreed.

A colorful headdress distinguishes a young Akha girl from her counterparts among the hill peoples of northern Thailand. As she grows older, the girl will add more decorations; when she reaches adulthood, she will adorn it with all the silver she can afford.

By 1976, the last U.S. air and naval units had departed.

Although Thailand was enacting radical changes, the country's new attitude was far from unanimous. Many senior military and civilian conservatives were anxious to undermine the civilian government so that the army could take over once more. A vicious reaction to the regime set in. Paramilitary groups of village thugs, some with the army or the police behind them, harassed the meetings of students and farmers. Dozens of politicians and labor leaders were assassinated.

The tactics succeeded. Early in 1976, the tensions within the ruling coalition forced Prime Minister Kukrit Pramoj to resign. The succeeding government was demoralized and unable to stem the rising tide of violence. Taking advantage of the chaos, 24 army officers staged a military coup against the elected government on October 6, 1976.

The year that followed the October 1976 coup was one of extraordinary political extremism by Thai standards. Farmers' and workers' groups were suppressed; there were political trials; books and newspapers were banned and burned. Many intellectuals sought refuge abroad; a few thousand students and others "went to the jungle" to join the Communist-led guerrillas, and the antigovernment insurrection renewed its intensity.

A more normal political climate was reestablished when a new generation of reformist army officers, known as the "Young Turks," promoted General Kriangsak to the premiership; then, in 1980, former commander in chief Prem Tinsulanond, another recently retired general, became premier. Soon after taking power, the latter offered the guerrillas an amnesty to return from the jungle to the cities. Thousands took up the offer, and the Communist party, simultaneously undermined by internal divisions and lack of external support, drastically declined in size and influence.

Prem introduced a largely civilian administration, which was far more liberal than any of its predecessors save those between 1973 and 1976. The army accepted the shift, albeit reluctantly. Military coups d'etat, almost biennial events in some postwar periods in Thailand, became rather less frequent and decidedly less successful. Some senior generals still claimed a mission to act as caretakers in the endlessly extended transition to democracy, but others began to advocate a more straightforward, professional role for the military.

Even under Prem's rule, Thailand remained a long way from democracy: Senior ministers were not required to be elected, and the Senate, the upper house of Parliament, was appointed. But the lower house was elected, and many were hopeful that by the mid-1980s the country was at last capable of moving toward a more genuinely parliamentary form of government.

More than 80 percent of Thailand's population lives in the countryside and pays little attention to political dramas played out in Bangkok. For centuries, village life has dominated Thai culture. Although the proportion of the agricultural labor force has declined from 88 percent in the early 1950s to less than 70 percent in the late 1980s, the number of farmers has increased with

On a misty morning, an Akha woman returns to her bamboo-and-thatch village with a basket of banana stems for her pigs. Like most of the other minorities inhabiting the hills of northern Thailand, the Akha have traditionally practiced an independent, seminomadic way of life.

6

Thailand's rapid population growth.

So far, Thailand has easily accommodated the burgeoning rural population, because vast tracts had never been cultivated until recently. In the late 1800s, about 50 percent of the land was forested, but the figure was below 20 percent by the late 1980s. The Thais have always been a relatively mobile people; when an area becomes crowded, a few inhabitants set off on their own and establish a new community on the forest fringe. One consequence of this pattern of settlement is that most Thai villages are less than 100 years old.

The pioneers look for a spot where wet-rice cultivation is possible, usually near a river. When they find it, they begin to settle themselves physically and spiritually in their forest abode. To them, the hills and the trees, the waters and the subsoil are the habitat of numerous spirits that must be exorcised, placated, or enlisted to help them in their practical endeavors. The Thais do not see this nature worship as distinct from their Buddhism. Some of their beliefs about the invisible beings around them probably originated in Thailand's pre-Buddhist days, but they have been effortlessly blended with Buddha's teachings.

Housebuilding, one of the villagers' first tasks, reveals their desire to achieve harmony with nature and to subdue it when possible. Auspicious times and locations for building are selected by experts, usually men who have served in a monastery for a while and can refer to textbooks on such matters. The timber chosen for the main house posts is freed of its spirit inhabitant by means of offerings and incantations and is given a soul and an honorific title. The floor of the house is built well off the ground to lift the dwellers away from insects, floods, and hostile spirits.

Traditional houses have bamboo or teak walls surrounded by wide verandas and a roof of braided leaves, grass, or wooden shingles. Although some walled rooms have doors, the main entrance to the house is not sealed by a

Workers turn out pencils in a factory outside Bangkok—a small-scale offshoot of Thailand's forest industry. Foreign demand for teak, coupled with domestic land clearance and consumption of timber for firewood, caused the country's forested area to be halved between 1961 and 1985.

door or other barrier, and there are only gaps for windows.

The village pioneers cut down and burn a patch of forest, and plant rice and vegetables on the plot they have created. Upon their death, the pioneers' land is divided equally between their sons and daughters; the next generation may in turn clear more land, probably farther from the village. In the meantime, married daughters live in their parents' homes with their husbands, sharing the work in the fields and house. Within the household, the women have considerable authority—more than in Malay societies—and they participate in most tasks.

In the past, villagers recall nostalgically, every household helped the others in building houses, planting, and harvesting the rice crop. Nowadays, the habit of cooperation is dwindling, but villagers still participate in one another's celebrations and rites of passage, not least by bringing food and cooking for numerous household feasts. Neighbors frequently visit one another to exchange news, banter, and expressions of affection.

Even the most casual visit is governed by decorous rules of politeness and etiquette. It is the host who must thank departing guests—rather than vice versa—for the honor of the visit. Great respect is accorded to elders; even a small age difference matters. The younger of two friends addresses the other as "older sibling" and is always careful to initiate the greeting.

Not long after a village is founded, the elders propose building a temple. Nobody is likely to demur, since constructing a place of worship and providing for monks are among the acts of piety thought to bring great spiritual merit, as well as social esteem, to the

An elephant lines up teak logs in a northern forest. Some 5,000 domesticated elephants work in Thailand's forest industry, hauling trees across ground too rough for machines. Several thousand wild elephants roam Thailand's national parks.

6

giver. Villagers are prepared to work extremely hard and make many material sacrifices for their shrine.

Initially, they may merely construct a hut with a fence around it for a monk to sleep in. Later, they will build a meeting hall and install an image of Buddha. If the community grows, the villagers will continue to expand the edifice, adding a sacred chapel and perhaps a cloister. There are celebrations to dedicate each stage and to attract contributions from villages far and wide. The householders provide the monks' daily food and the necessities for the year-round succession of holy days.

Those who enter the temple community as monks are villagers themselves, albeit elevated to a sacred status by the ritual of ordination. Some may remain members of the Buddhist order of monks for several years, or even all their lives. Most, however, serve only

for a three-month period once in their lives, perhaps just before marriage. Often they choose the rainy season—the growing period for the main rice crop—when there is little work in the fields. The decision is up to the individual, who may leave at any time.

The temple is central to the lives of all the villagers. They go there to listen to the scriptures, to make vows and offerings, and also to discuss secular matters. It is in the sacred compound that processional floats for festivals are made, and that drums and gongs are stored and practiced. Some monks may have expertise in giving medical, astrological, or other counsel. They are available to perform domestic rituals, chanting scriptures in the house of the dead and leading the funeral bier to the cremation ground.

Villages are no longer isolated from the outside world the way they were as

recently as the 1960s. Buses and trucks allow most villagers to make a day trip to the nearest market town, where once the journey might have taken a week. In town, government influence will be present in the form of the district office, which houses land records, the registry of births, marriages, and deaths, and the army recruiting office.

Other urban influences have begun to change the look of Thai villages. Many houses now have doors with locks and shuttered windows; the wealthy build two-story homes of brick. Young people generally wear Western dress. Electricity has reached some communities, and the well-to-do own fans, refrigerators, and television sets. Village committees and offices proliferate according to bewildering ministerial plans. Where once there might only have been groups concerned with the temple and perhaps irrigation, there

are now bodies supervising schools and land development, farming cooperatives, defense volunteers, and organizations for young people.

While the intrusion of the state and the market into agrarian life has in a sense drawn rural people into a closer relationship with national society, it has also created new gulfs within the villages themselves. Two decades of planned development have created a new local elite of officeholders, traders, building contractors, moneylenders, landlords, and owners of trucks and agricultural machinery. Starting off with only a little more than their neighbors in terms of property or office, they have capitalized on the greatly increased opportunities for trading and hobnobbing with officials. Members of this group predominate in the committees and often take the law into their own hands when dealing with less well-off neighbors. Thai traditions of deference to those higher up in the hierarchy bolster their power.

Many escape rural poverty and dependence by seeking work elsewhere. Some villages, especially in the northeast, seem to contain only the children and the old who have been left behind. Those Thais who can scrape together the money for traveling and labor-brokers' fees head for the Middle East, Malaysia, or Singapore. In some years, the value of the annual remittances of Thais working abroad equals that of the entire rice export. The alternative is to head for the towns. Most urban workers are first- or second-generation peasants. Bangkok, where industry and commerce are concentrated, is the goal for the majority.

The capital has a population of more than five million and is 20 times larger than the next biggest city—Chiang Mai,

in the north. Built on both sides of the Chao Phraya River, Bangkok is crisscrossed with canals that annually flood the streets and ground floors of houses. In the past there were many more canals, but the majority have been filled in and transformed into roads. Even so, traffic problems still plague the city. In the streets, rickshaw drivers compete for survival with innumerable small trucks bringing market produce from the surrounding country, with buses packed to overflowing, and with the air-conditioned, black-windowed, chauffeur-driven limousines of the privileged few. Only the imminent passage of a royal procession—in white or yellow Daimlers and Mercedes—produces a respectful hush. The streets are cleared and construction workers urged to descend from their scaffolding, more to avoid the impropriety of being higher than the king than for security reasons.

The many fine temples and palaces, old ministerial buildings in classical European style, and rows of shops with living space above, which were the chief architectural features of the city until the 1960s, have been overshadowed by massive new office buildings, hotels, and shopping centers. But the main thoroughfares are still filled with tens of thousands of street vendors.

Some hawk their goods from place to place. Food vendors maneuver bicycles adapted to carry large display cabinets and huge umbrellas. Indians carry trays of assorted nuts on their heads; Chinese peddle steamed muffins and fried soybean curd. Others set up stalls outside shops, along canals, or under elevated highways, strongly resisting periodic attempts by officials to drive them off the streets in the interests of tidying up the capital. Among them are

sun-darkened villagers in brightly colored sarongs and broad-brimmed farmers' hats who have traveled in for the day by bus or truck. They carry what they can—including, if necessary, a charcoal stove—in two baskets slung at either end of a springy bamboo shoulder pole. There is an occasional astrologer or a young northeasterner selling traditional cushions, but most vendors cater to the Thais' fondness for snacks. They sell rice delicacies wrapped in banana leaves or cooked in bamboo tubes, hot cakes freshly baked on charcoal, flattened dried squid, hot spicy noodles. And they capitalize on the wonderful variety of fresh fruit found throughout the region, offering juice, preserved fruits, mangoes with rice and coconut cream, or pineapple served with the crushed ice that seems to be available everywhere.

Some of the first-generation city-dwellers survive even more precariously than the street vendors. More than one million children between the ages of 7 and 11 are engaged in production, often in small urban sweatshops. Thousands stay alive scavenging in garbage dumps or recycling discarded bags and bottles. Figures for female prostitution in Thailand range from half a million to double that amount, of which a large fraction is in Bangkok.

Thai society has always condoned prostitution, but it was in the Vietnam War years, when thousands of servicemen passed through on rest and recreation trips, that sex became big business. Now it has become a key ingredient in Thailand's appeal to tourists. Relishing the foreign exchange it draws in, the authorities have turned a blind eye to the night life of Bangkok and the other cities, giving scant thought to the social costs. Most

Rush-hour traffic chokes a street in Bangkok, which accommodates 90 percent of the motor vehicles in Thailand. To ease congestion, the government has initiated a beltway system, an elevated expressway, and an overhead railroad.

143

6

A Thai Muslim—a member of the country's largest religious minority—walks past ornately decorated fishing boats beached outside a village on the southeast coast. Fish, mainly mackerel, accounts for more than half the protein in the national diet.

144

of the prostitutes are under 18, and 1 in 10 is less than 13 years old. Most come from distant villages and are at the mercy of the pimps who recruit them as they alight from the trains into the cities. Some become virtual slaves, getting little beyond their meager meals.

Not all the newcomers to the cities fall into desperate straits. Many find real opportunities for advancement. The economic growth of the past three decades has created thousands of jobs in retailing, service industries, computers, and many other fields. Those who have taken advantage of the openings and groomed their children for higher positions are rapidly swelling the ranks of the middle class, which traditionally was a very limited group, composed of Chinese entrepreneurs and Thai officials. Increasingly educated and well traveled, the members of today's middle class admire Western habits and institutions. Their clothes and possessions are Western, though they retain their Buddhism and ingrained habits of politeness and deference.

Members of the burgeoning middle class are frustrated by Thailand's highly personalized politics, which leaves their own views little scope for expression. They aspire to succeed the generals in power and to introduce a civilian democratic polity. Until a *modus vivendi* is established between these educated, articulate dissenters and the army, Thai politics will lack stability. But whatever the outcome of today's uncertainties, the future will surely be marked by the grace and endurance of the Thai people.

The same qualities may aid Thailand in its quest for peace with its neighbors. Thailand can never afford to forget that it is a frontline state, facing the potentially belligerent Vietnamese across its eastern border. But the country that collaborated with the Japanese during World War II and still managed to end the war on good terms with the Allies has not lost its nimbleness. Today, it attempts cordial relations with powers of every political stripe. Although they left their bases in 1976, the Americans have supplied military aid ever since the Vietnamese invasion of Kampuchea in 1979. And since 1975, relations with China have been warm.

But perhaps the most valued of Thailand's friends are its partners in ASEAN. Culturally, the Thais, with their monarchy, religion, and history of feuds with the Vietnamese, are some distance from the other ASEAN nations. On the other hand, Thailand has had no quarrel with any other ASEAN country, whereas several of them had been at loggerheads until recently.

The country has yet to benefit substantially from the tentative attempts at economic cooperation within ASEAN, and there is no guarantee that any of the other countries would come to Thailand's aid if it was invaded. Yet it is these countries who most closely share Thailand's interests; Thailand feels stronger and more secure because of its links with neighboring non-Communist countries in an explosive part of the world. It has long been accepted in ASEAN that special weight should be given to the views of Thailand—its only frontline state—in formulating diplomatic policy. And Thailand needs support from its neighbors. The 1979 invasion of Kampuchea is a notable example of the ASEAN members' collective strength in condemning destabilizing forces in the region. Ever pragmatic and increasingly cooperative, the countries of ASEAN face their destiny with courage and optimism. □

Novices with shaved heads line up at
the temple steps to receive food from
passing worshipers. Under normal
circumstances, the monks must go
into town with their bowls to seek
alms, but this is a Buddhist festival
day, and townspeople will throng
Haripunchai's compound to pray.

146

MONASTIC LIFE IN THAILAND

The ancient Buddhist temple of Haripunchai is the greatest treasure of the town of Lamphun in northern Thailand. Like its counterparts across the nation, Haripunchai draws its monks from the local populace; it is normally home to a brotherhood of about 40 adults and 70 novices, teenagers attending the temple school. After a few months or years, most will return to the outside world.

The monks see their sojourn in the temple as an opportunity to strive for perfection. Buddhism teaches that reincarnation follows death, and that only by living according to the highest standards can a person ever escape the wearisome round of death and rebirth. Recognizing how hard it is for a layperson to obey such maxims as never harming another creature, most Thai men enter a monastery at least once in their lives. Their laybrethren express their own religious feelings by supporting the monks with gifts.

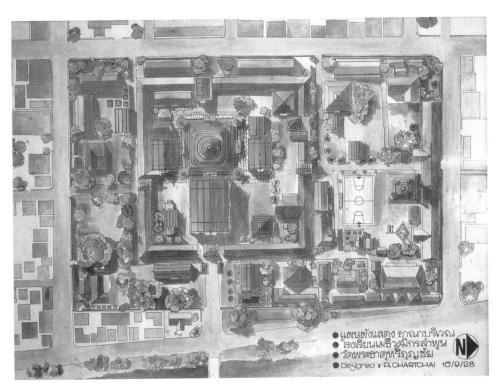

A plan of Haripunchai executed by a teacher in the temple school illustrates a typical disposition of temple buildings. The monks' quarters and the classrooms are on the perimeter. Holy structures, including the *chedi*— a spire that enshrines a relic of Buddha—are found in the central area.

Young monks pass in front of the sacred *chedi*, the oldest building in the temple. Its base dates back to the 10th or 11th century; the bell-shaped dome of burnished copper was rebuilt several times in later centuries.

In the incense-laden chiaroscuro of the prayer hall, a lone worshiper kneels before images of Buddha. His solitary act of devotion is characteristic of Buddhism's emphasis on inwardness: Although the monks pray together each evening, communal worship for laypeople is rare.

149

At the temple school (*below*), novices and laychildren share a classroom. Unlike state-run secondary education, the school at Haripunchai is free. Three quarters of the pupils live here or in other nearby monasteries; the rest come in each day from the town.

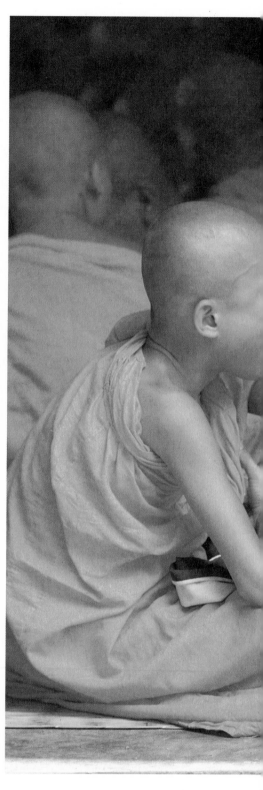

Soon after dawn, a woman bows to show her respect for alms-seeking monks who have accepted her gift of rice. Regular givers know the monks' routes and wait in the same spot daily with their contributions.

Young novices pool their gifts of food for a communal meal. Inmates may eat only between sunrise and noon; they normally have one meal on their return from their dawn alms-collection rounds and another at the end of the morning.

At a private ceremony in Lamphun, chanting monks bless the house, its owner, her dead parents, and all her ancestors. The far end of the cord invests a bowl of holy water with their prayers. Some of the water will be sprinkled over the guests, and the rest kept by the householder.

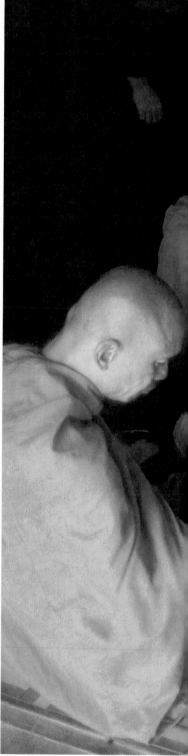

Once the ceremony is over, the monks sit down to a lavish meal, prepared by the householder as recompense for their services. Having gained spiritual merit through their holy ministrations, she is expected to pay accordingly for the benefits.

Within the temple compound, a young monk and his companions bask in the afternoon sun. Monks are not confined to their quarters: As long as they are present for meals, prayers, and lessons, they are free to wander in the town as they please.

PICTURE CREDITS

Credits from left to right are separated by semicolons, from top to bottom by dashes.

Cover: Juergen Schmitt from The Image Bank, London. Front endpaper: Map by Roger Stewart, London. Back endpaper: Digitized map by Ralph Scott/Chapman Bounford, London.

1, 2: © Flag Research Center, Winchester, Massachusetts. 6, 7: Graham Grieves from Robert Harding Picture Library, London, digitized images by Ralph Scott/Chapman Bounford, London (2)—John Drummond. 8, 9: Amos Schliack from Focus, Hamburg, digitized image by Ralph Scott/Chapman Bounford, London. 10, 11: Michael Freeman, London, digitized image by Ralph Scott/Chapman Bounford, London. 12, 13: Hans Hoefer from APA Photo Agency, Singapore. 14-17: Michael Freeman, London. 18: Michael Freeman, London; Barbara Gundle, Portland, Oregon; Marlane Guelden, Kuala Lumpur. 19: Michael Freeman, London; Vautier-de-Nanxe, Paris; Michael Freeman, London. 20: Vautier-de-Nanxe, Paris. 21: Michael MacIntyre from The Hutchison Library, London. 22: Rainer Drexel from Bilderberg, Hamburg. 25: Hans Hoefer from APA Photo Agency, Singapore. 26: Lyle Lawson, London. 28: "Opperkoopman voc & retourboot op de rede van Batavia" by Aelbert Cuyp, courtesy of the Rijksmuseum, Amsterdam. 29: Michael Freeman, London. 30: Anne Conway, Paris. 31: Courtesy the Imperial War Museum, London. 32, 33: J. Henebry, Wilmette, Illinois. 34: Amos Schliack from Focus, Hamburg. 36: Michael Freeman, London. 37: Dr. Georg Gerster from The John Hillelson Picture Agency, London. 38, 39: Joseph Viesti from Agence ANA, Paris. 40: Kal Müller from APA Photo Agency, Singapore. 41: Michael Freeman, London. 42: Courtesy the Victoria and Albert Museum, London (IM 147-1921); "Iacatara (Djakarta)" from *Livro do estado da India Oriental*, 1646, courtesy The British Library, London; Paul Conklin from Camera Press, London. 44: Sybil Sassoon from Robert Harding Picture Library, London. 46: Michael Freeman, London. 47: G. P. Reichelt, Hamburg. 49: Vautier-de-Nanxe, Paris—Sybil Sassoon from Robert Harding Picture Library, London. 50, 51: D. and J. Heaton from Colorific!, London. 53: Sybil Sassoon from Robert Harding Picture Library, London. 54: Vautier-de-Nanxe, Paris. 55: Gregory Lawler, Portland, Oregon. 56, 57: John Egan, The Hutchison Library, London. 58-67: Michael Freeman, London. 68: David Liddle from Horizon International Photographic Agency, Sydney. 69: Lyle Lawson, London. 70, 71: Anthony Howarth from Susan Griggs Agency, London. 72: Lyle Lawson, London—Gunther Deichmann, Darwin, Australia (2). 73: Michael Freeman, London. 74, 75: Amos Schliack from Focus, Hamburg. 77: "Alfonso de Albuquerque" from *Livro do estado da India Oriental*, 1646, courtesy of The British Library, London; detail, oil on canvas by F. Grant, 1847, courtesy The National Portrait Gallery, London; Map Research Center, Winchester, Massachusetts—Courtesy the National Maritime Museum, London. 78: Margaret Collier from Robert Harding Picture Library, London. 79: Michael Freeman, London. 80: David Alan Harvey from Woodfin Camp Inc., Washington, D.C. 81: Lance Nelson from Horizon International Photographic Agency, Sydney. 82: Michael Freeman, London. 83: David Alan Harvey from Susan Griggs Agency, London. 85: Raghubir Singh from Agence ANA, Paris. 86, 87: Lyle Lawson, London. 88: Adam Woolfitt from Susan Griggs Agency, London. 89: R. Ian Lloyd from APA Photo Agency, Singapore. 90, 91: Patrick Ward, London. 92: detail, oil on canvas by G. F. Joseph, 1817, courtesy The National Portrait Gallery, London. 93: Lithograph by J. T. Thompson, photo by Philip Little from APA Photo Agency, Singapore. 94: R. Ian Lloyd from APA Photo Agency, Singapore. 96: Michael Freeman, London. 97-99: Adam Woolfitt from Susan Griggs Agency, London. 100, 101: Michael Freeman, London. 102: Piers Cavendish from Reflex Picture Agency, London. 103: Christopher Bain, Port Washington, New York. 104: Alain Evrard from Susan Griggs Agency, London. 105: Professor Charles Boxer, Little Gaddensden, Hertfordshire, England; courtesy *Punch*, London—Piers Cavendish from Reflex Picture Agency, London. 106-109: Michael Freeman, London. 110, 111: Ted Spiegel from Susan Griggs Agency, London. 112: Piers Cavendish from Reflex Picture Agency, London. 115: Harald Sund, Seattle, Washington. 116, 117: Robert Frerck from Odyssey Productions, Chicago, Illinois. 118-130: Michael Freeman, London. 131: Gunther Deichmann, Darwin, Australia. 132: Michael Freeman, London. 134: Ann and Bury Peerless, Birchington-on-Sea, Kent, England. 135: Werner Forman Archive, London; "King Mongkut" from *Louis and the King of Siam* by Dr. W. S. Bristowe, courtesy Mrs. Belinda Brocklehurst, Tunbridge Wells, Kent, England. 136-139: Michael Freeman, London. 140: Jean Guy Jules from Agence ANA, Paris. 141: Jim Howard from Colorific!, London. 142: Amos Schliack from Focus, Hamburg. 144, 145: Lyle Lawson, London. 146-155: Michael Freeman, London.

ACKNOWLEDGMENTS

The index for this book was prepared by Vicki Robinson. For their assistance in the preparation of this volume, the editors express their gratitude to the following people and institutions: The abbot of Wat Phrathat Haripunchai, Lamphun, Thailand; Sonny Aguirre, Manila; Guy Andrews, London; Judy Aspinall, London; British Council for Aid to Refugees, London; Mike Brown, London; Siriporn Buranaphan, Bangkok; Kate Cann, Guildford, Surrey, England; Inson Charoenporn, Chiang Mai, Thailand; Helen R. Chauncey, Department of History, Georgetown University, Washington, D.C.; Windsor Chorlton, London; Alan Croghan, USIS, U.S. Embassy, Manila; A. Dewey, Total Oil, London; Constante N. Firme, M.D., Dr. José Fabella Memorial Hospital, Manila; Felicia Freeland, London; Friends of the Earth, London; Cherrie Gross, London; Helen Grubin, London; Andy Hernandes, Manila; Barbara Moir Hicks, London; Joanna Hucker, London; Shuib Hussain, Tourist Development Corporation, Penang, Malaysia; Indonesian Embassy, London; International Press Center, Manila; Isra Jerachaisakdecha, Chiang Mai, Thailand; Lieutenant Daniel P. Lachica, 20th Air Commando Squadron, Villamor Air Base, Pasay City, Philippines; Cindy Lilles, Manila Hotel, Manila; R. A. Longmire, Bookham, Surrey, England; Malaysian High Commission, London; Carla and Davide Manfreddi, Bali; R. W. Sasminta Mardawa, Jogjakarta, Indonesia; Anton Neumann, London; Mary Beth Oelkers-Keegan, Alexandria, Virginia; Susan Ooi, London; Captain Norbie Panganiban, 20th Air Commando Squadron, Villamore Air Base, Pasay City, Philippines; Roy Perrott, London; Elizabeth Plint, Oxford, England; Prince G. P. Poeroeboyo, Jogjakarta, Indonesia; Sally Rowland, Saffron Walden, Essex, England; Andrew Sarao, Manila; Asad Shiraz, Singapore Tourist Promotion Board, Singapore; Singapore High Commission, London; Singapore Tourist Promotion Board, London; Grace de Solo, Manila; Sri Sultan Hamengkubuwono IX of Jogjakarta; Colette Stockum, Alexandria, Virginia; Tjokorda Gde Putra Sukawati, Bali; Pichai Suranantsri, Bangkok; Agus Suwito, Jogjakarta, Indonesia; David Tan, London; Thai Embassy, London; Tourism Authority of Thailand, Bangkok; Sandro Tucci, Manila; Bodge Wallingford, Chiang Mai, Thailand; Apichart Weerawong, Bangkok.

BIBLIOGRAPHY

BOOKS

Allen, Charles, *Tales from the South China Seas.* London: British Broadcasting Corporation, André Deutsch, 1983.

Andaya, Barbara J. Watson, and Leonard Y. Andaya, *A History of Malaysia.* London: The Macmillan Press, 1982.

Anima, Nid, *In Defense of Cockfighting.* Quezon City, Philippines: Omar Publications, 1977.

Asia 1985 Yearbook. Hong Kong: Far Eastern Economic Review, 1985.

Bedlington, Stanley S., *Malaysia and Singapore.* London: Cornell University Press, 1978.

Bunge, Frederica M., ed.:

Malaysia: A Country Study. Foreign Area Studies, The American University, Washington, D.C., 1984.

Philippines: A Country Study. Washington, D.C.: Foreign Area Studies, The American University, 1984.

Thailand: A Country Study. Washington, D.C.: Foreign Area Studies, The American University, 1981.

Bunnag, Jane, *Buddhist Monk, Buddhist Layman: A Study of Urban Monastic Organisation in Central Thailand.* Cambridge: Cambridge University Press, 1973.

Choy, Lee Khoon, *Indonesia: Between Myth and Reality.* London: Nile & Mackenzie, 1976.

Constantino, Renato, *A History of the Philippines.* New York and London: Monthly Review Press, 1975.

Dalton, Bill, *Indonesia Handbook.* Chico, California: Moon Publications, 1980.

Dutt, Ashok K., ed., *Southeast Asia—Realm of Contrasts.* Boulder, Colorado: Westview Press, 1985.

Farmer, B. H., *An Introduction to South Asia.* London: Methuen & Company, 1983.

Fisher, Charles A., *South-East Asia, a Social, Economic and Political Geography.* London: Methuen & Company, 1964.

Flower, Raymond, *Raffles: The Story of Singapore.* Kent: Croom Helm, 1984.

Geertz, Clifford, *Agricultural Involution: Indonesia.* Berkeley, California: University of California Press, 1963.

Gorospe, Vitaliano R., and Richard L. Deats, *The Filipino in the Seventies.* Quezon City, Philippines: New Day Publishers, 1973.

Grant, Bruce, *Indonesia.* London: Cambridge University Press, 1964.

Haditjaroko, Sunardjo, *Ramayana, Indonesia Wayang Show.* Jakarta: Penerbit Djambatari, 1981.

Hanks, Lucien M., *Rice & Man: Ecology in Southeast Asia.* Chicago: Aldine Atterton, 1972.

Hunter, Guy, *South-East Asia—Race, Culture and Nation.* Kuala Lumpur: Oxford University Press, 1966.

Indonesia (Insight Guide). Singapore: Apa Productions, 1985.

The Japanese Occupation: Singapore 1942-1945. Singapore: Archives and Oral History Department, News and Publication, 1985.

Jocano, F. Landa, *Slum as a Way of Life.* Quezon City, Philippines: University of the Philippines Press, 1975.

Josey, Alex, *Singapore: Its Past, Present and Future.* London: André Deutsch, 1980.

Kaleidoscope: Indonesia Meeting the 21st Century. Hong Kong: Eurasia Media Company, 1984.

Khoo, Gilbert, *A History of South-East Asia since 1500.* Kuala Lumpur: Oxford University Press, 1970.

Legge, J. D., *Sukarno: A Political Biography.* Allen Lane, London: The Penguin Press, 1972.

Lewis, Elaine, and Paul Lewis, *Peoples of the Golden Triangle, Six Tribes in Thailand.* London: Thames and Hudson, 1984.

Malaysia (Insight Guide). Singapore: Apa Productions, 1985.

Miller, Russell, and the Editors of Time-Life Books, *The East Indiamen* (The Seafarers series). Alexandria, Virginia: Time-Life Books, 1980.

Moebirman, *Wayang Purwa, the Shadow Play of Indonesia.* Jakarta: Yayasan Pelita Wisata, 1973.

Nelson, Raymond, *The Philippines.* London: Thames and Hudson, 1968.

Osborne, Milton, *Southeast Asia: An Introductory History.* London: George Allen & Unwin, 1979.

Palmier, Leslie, *Indonesia.* London: Thames and Hudson, 1965.

Philippines (Insight Guide). Singapore: Apa Productions, 1984.

Ricklefs, Merle C., *A History of Modern Indonesia.* London: The Macmillan Press, 1981.

Ryan, Neil J., *A History of Malaysia and Singapore.* Kuala Lumpur: Oxford University Press, 1976.

Scoble, Henry M., and Laurie S. Wiseberg, eds., *Access to Justice: Human Rights Struggles in South East Asia.* London: Zed Books, 1985.

Sien, Chia Lin, and Colin MacAndrews, eds., *Southeast Asian Seas, Frontiers for Development.* Singapore: McGraw-Hill International Book Company, 1981.

Sievers, Allen M., *The Mystical World of Indonesia: Culture and Economic Development in Conflict.* Baltimore: The Johns Hopkins University Press, 1974.

Singapore (Insight Guide). Singapore: Apa Productions, 1984.

Steinberg, David Joel, ed., *In Search of Southeast Asia.* London: Praeger Publishers, 1971.

Steinberg, Rafael, and the Editors of Time-Life Books, *Return to the Philippines* (World War II series). Alexandria, Virginia: Time-Life Books, 1979.

Sutlive, J. R., and H. Vinson, *The Iban of Sarawak.* Illinois: AHM Publishing Corporation, 1978.

Taylor, John Gelman, *The Social World of Batavia: European and Eurasian in Dutch Asia.* Madison, Wisconsin: The University of Wisconsin Press, 1983.

Thailand (Insight Guide). Singapore: Apa Productions, 1985.

Thailand Angkor (Cambodia). Geneva: Nagel, 1973.

Thailand into the 80s. Bangkok: Published by the Office of the Prime Minister, 1980.

Torres, Emmanuel, *Jeepney.* Quezon City, Philippines: GCF Books, 1979.

Vreeland, Nena, *Area Handbook for Singapore.* Washington, D.C.: Foreign Area Studies, The American University, 1977.

Wheeler, Tony, *South-East Asia on a Shoestring.* South Yarra, Victoria, Australia: Lonely Planet Publications, 1985.

World Development Report 1984. New York: The World Bank, Oxford University Press, 1984.

Zich, Arthur, and the Editors of Time-Life Books, *The Rising Sun* (World War II series). Alexandria, Virginia: Time-Life Books, 1977.

PERIODICALS

"Alike But Different," *Far Eastern Economic Review,* April 18, 1985.

"Ancient Magic," *Connoisseur,* November 1985.

"Asean," *The Times,* April 30, 1984.

"The Chinese in Indonesia, the Philippines and Malaysia," *Minority Rights Group,* Report No. 10, revised 1982 edition.

"File on the Philippines," *Departures,* January-February 1985.

"The Filipinos," *Asiaweek,* November 29, 1985.

"Indonesia," *Financial Times,* April 30, 1984.

"Indonesia: Suharto Steps Out," *The World Today,* October 1985.

"The Malaysians," *Asiaweek,* May 10, 1985.

"Monsoons," *National Geographic,* December 1984.

"The Philippines Search for Identity," *Asian Affairs,* October 1985.

"Poverty in Indonesia," *World Bank Staff Working Papers,* no. 671, 1984.

"Singapore," *Financial Times,* December 12, 1984.

"Singapore's Success Story," *New Leader,* August 12, 1985.

"The Strange Case of Singapore," *Geo,* November 1984.

"A Test for Democracy," *Time,* February 3, 1986.

"West Irian, East Timor and Indonesia," *Minority Rights Group,* Report No. 42, 1979.

INDEX

Page numbers in italics refer to an illustration of the subject mentioned.

Time-Life Books Inc. offers a wide range of fine recordings, including a *Rock 'n' Roll Era* series. For subscription information, call 1-800-621-7026, or write TIME-LIFE MUSIC, P. O. Box C-32068, Richmond, Virginia 23261-2068.

CHINA

BURMA

LAOS

Mae Hong Son

Chiang Mai
Lamphun

Sukhothai

THAILAND

HONG KON

Ayutthaya
Thonburi   **Bangkok**
Damnoen Saduak

KAMPUCHEA

VIETNAM

SOUTH CHINA SEA

PALAW

Kota Bharu

PENANG   George Town

MALAYA

Medan

Kota Kinabalu

Bandar Seri Begawan   **SABA**

BRUNEI

Kuala Lumpur

Rantau   Malacca

SINGAPORE

Jurong

MALAYSIA

SARAWAK

Kuching

KALIMANTAN

Padang

SUMATRA

Palembang

JAVA SEA

Jakarta

INDIAN OCEAN

Bandung

Borobudur   *JAVA*   Surabaya
Prambanan   Surakarta (Solo)
Jogjakarta   *BALI*   *SUMBA*
Ubud

LOMBOK